Comparative Approaches to Compassion

Also available from Bloomsbury:

Andean Aesthetics and Anticolonial Resistance, by Omar Rivera
Chinese and Indian Ways of Thinking in Early Modern European Philosophy, by Selusi Ambrogio
Indian and Intercultural Philosophy, by Douglas L. Berger
Interpreting Chinese Philosophy, by Jana S. Rošker
Nonviolent Resistance as a Philosophy of Life, by Ramin Jahanbegloo

Comparative Approaches to Compassion

Understanding Nonviolence in World Religions and Politics

Ramin Jahanbegloo

BLOOMSBURY ACADEMIC
LONDON · NEW YORK · OXFORD · NEW DELHI · SYDNEY

BLOOMSBURY ACADEMIC
Bloomsbury Publishing Plc
50 Bedford Square, London, WC1B 3DP, UK
1385 Broadway, New York, NY 10018, USA
29 Earlsfort Terrace, Dublin 2, Ireland

BLOOMSBURY, BLOOMSBURY ACADEMIC and the Diana logo are
trademarks of Bloomsbury Publishing Plc

First published in Great Britain 2022
This paperback edition published 2023

Copyright © Ramin Jahanbegloo, 2022

Ramin Jahanbegloo has asserted his right under the Copyright,
Designs and Patents Act, 1988, to be identified as Author of this work.

Cover image: REUTERS / Alamy Stock Photo

All rights reserved. No part of this publication may be reproduced or transmitted
in any form or by any means, electronic or mechanical, including photocopying,
recording, or any information storage or retrieval system, without prior
permission in writing from the publishers.

Bloomsbury Publishing Plc does not have any control over, or responsibility for,
any third-party websites referred to or in this book. All internet addresses given
in this book were correct at the time of going to press. The author and publisher
regret any inconvenience caused if addresses have changed or sites have ceased
to exist, but can accept no responsibility for any such changes.

A catalogue record for this book is available from the British Library.

A catalog record for this book is available from the Library of Congress.

ISBN:	HB:	978-1-3502-8886-7
	PB:	978-1-3502-8890-4
	ePDF:	978-1-3502-8887-4
	eBook:	978-1-3502-8888-1

Typeset by Integra Software Services Pvt. Ltd.

To find out more about our authors and books visit www.bloomsbury.com
and sign up for our newsletters.

In the memory of my teacher
Pierre-Jean Labarrière

Contents

Introduction: Human Fragility and Compassion	1
1 *Ahimsa* in Jainism, Buddhism, and Hinduism: A Compassionate View of Life	19
2 Love and Compassion in Christianity: From Jesus Christ to Thomas Merton	33
3 Mahatma Gandhi: Compassionate Citizenship and Feminization of Politics	55
4 The Twin Heritage of Gandhian Nonviolence: Martin Luther King, Jr. and Khan Abdul Ghaffar Khan	69
5 Toward a Compassionate Civilization: From *Swaraj* to *The Beloved Community*	85
6 Nelson Mandela: Common Humanity and Ethics of Empathy	101
Conclusion: Spiritualizing Compassion and Nonviolence	113
Notes	143
Bibliography	157
Index	162

Introduction: Human Fragility and Compassion

Man is a fragile animal. This fragility is not only biological, due to the fact that human beings die, but also ontological, in relation to everyday existence of individuals as members of a fragile species. However, what makes the huge difference between a human being and animals is that the former is totally conscious about its fragility as a living being. Man is a fragile being who cannot, in any circumstances, step beyond his fragility. At the same time, every individual, as a fragile being, realizes, at every moment of its life, that it cannot not think about its own fragility without thinking about the fragility of others. Life, in all and for all, consists in learning that humanity is fragile. This means basically learning who we are: *homo fragilis*, and what we can do with this fragility. Undoubtedly this ontological dimension of fragility is the foundation of our relatedness to others which appears in the form of love. As Kierkegaard puts it, "No human being can place the ground of love in another person's heart; yet love is the ground, and we build up only from the ground up; therefore, we can build up only by presupposing love. Take love away—then there is no one who builds up and no one who is built up."[1] If there is search for love in human beings, it is because fragility creates a need for interconnectedness. To search for love is to presuppose fragility in oneself. To give one's love to others is to presuppose that they are

2   *Comparative Approaches to Compassion*

also fragile, but capable of nursing and healing our fragility. The ontological fragility of human beings is not a being-for-oneself quality, but a quality by which we give our love to others. As Thomas Merton affirms:

> Love is, in fact, an intensification of life, a completeness, a fullness, a wholeness of life. We do not live merely in order to vegetate through our days until we die. Nor do we live merely in order to take part in the routines of work and amusement that go on around us. We are not just machines that have to be cared for and driven carefully until they run down. In other words, life is not a straight horizontal line between two points, birth and death.... We do not become fully human until we give ourselves to each other in love.[2]

What Merton is pointing out is that the center of gravity of *homo fragilis* is a philosophy of love. Man is uplifted by love because he needs to compensate his fragility with a search for spiritual fulfillment. Love can change our mind and our body, which are both determined by our fragility. Love, also, tames our savage ego, which considers the world as its own conquest. Truly, Man is a conqueror, because Man is weak and fragile. To conquer is a way for humankind to conceal its ontological fragility. But *homo fragilis* is a spiritual animal which creates meaning, and love is an expression of spirituality. "Love," proclaims Kierkegaard, "is the source of everything and, in the spiritual sense, love is the deepest ground of the spiritual life. In every human being in whom there is love, the foundation, in the spiritual sense, is laid. And the building that, in the spiritual sense, is to be erected is again love, and it is love that builds up."[3]

Love is the development of the spiritual in life. Love is the source of happiness in human beings. But more important, it gives meaning to life itself. Love is the inner essence of everything. As such, the world is nothing but the objectification of love. There is no world without the love of the world (*Amor Mundi*). Of course, the reference here is not to "romantic" or "sexual" love, which is a common feeling which is practiced privately. *Amor Mundi* is not a private or romantic love. It is the principal moving force which drives all living creatures on Earth. As long as life has a meaning for the humankind, human beings can go on living and creating. As such, life is not only a biological adventure for humankind, but it is also an ontological effort of giving meaning to the surrounding world. It is not enough to live in order to have a meaningful life. If that were true, life would have been simple. But seeking the meaning of life is more complex than it appears: it is a battle which is waged within the essence of life itself. There are no prayers which can spare us from living a shallow life. We cannot hope to receive a gift of thinking from the gods, while we continue living a meaningless life. No doubt, a compassionate life is a meaningful mode of existing. As Milan Kundera writes in his novel, *The Unbearable Lightness of Being*, "there is nothing heavier than compassion. Not even one's own pain weighs so heavy as the pain one feels with someone, for someone, a pain intensified by the imagination and prolonged by a hundred echoes."[4]

It is interesting up to what degree human civilization has functioned as a process of concealment of human fragility and the quest of *homo fragilis* for the domination of the world under the banner of progress and freedom. Only the history of humanity can reveal the depth of this domination, exemplified by the massive destruction of biodiversity and cultural diversity in modern times. To be sure, the ontological fragility of humankind turned out to be a ferocious enemy for the "otherness of the Other." Today,

4   *Comparative Approaches to Compassion*

after 5,000 years of war, violence, domination, and destruction, humankind is proud of having turned the Earth into hell. As Marcuse argues:

> [T]he capability to overkill and to overburn, and the mental behavior that goes with it are by-products of the development of the productive forces within a system of exploitation and repression; they seem to become more productive the more comfortable the system becomes to its privileged subjects. The affluent society has now demonstrated that it is a society at war; if its citizens have not noticed it, its victims certainly have.[5]

To be sure, the extreme violence practiced by human civilization in different periods of its "progress" shows well that humankind has never succeeded in totally mastering its desire for violence and domination. Moreover, the civilizational need to progress, as a conscious mode of denying human fragility, continues to haunt today's technocratic and corporate mindset, which tries to liberate itself from the past crimes and atrocities of human history and move toward a radiant future which glorifies a happiness with no memory.

As a matter of fact, the civilizational experience of *homo fragilis* has turned out to be a disappointing experience for the humankind, except in its quest for wisdom and nonviolence through art, philosophy, and spirituality. Of course, it goes without saying that the capacity to create beauty and to attain the moral higher grounds has never been a virtue of the masses. If we speak about political, economic, or cultural fragility in our contemporary societies, we need also to ask whether the spiritual structure of these societies is conducive to a level of ethical and aesthetic education of individuals. However, no critical observer of these societies can doubt that the ability to practice selfless love,

Introduction 5

compassion, and empathy is a rare phenomenon and considered as non-utilitarian. Although the world is tied together by economic, political, and technological ties, the level of responsibility to and for other human beings and other living creatures has decreased. Simply because, as Thomas Merton argues correctly:

> The insistence on always having what you want, on always being satisfied, on always being fulfilled, makes love impossible. To love you have to climb out of the cradle, where everything is "getting", and grow up to the maturity of giving, without concern for getting anything special in return. Love is not a deal, it is a sacrifice. It is not marketing, it is a form of worship.[6]

Merton is not referring here to erotic or romantic love, but to a compassionate and empathetic love that understands the otherness of the other person. The otherness of the Other is the strangeness of the stranger. As it is said in *Deuteronomy 10:19*, "Ye shall love the stranger; for ye have been strangers in the land of Egypt." To love a stranger is to respect him/her as a stranger, but also to feel responsible for him/her. To respect and to be responsible is to be responsive. To be responsive to the otherness of the Other is, therefore, to identify oneself with the Other and share their suffering. But it would be wrong to take this attitude of responsiveness and experience of shared suffering for granted. As Fromm puts it, "Today responsibility is often meant to denote duty, something imposed upon one from outside. But responsibility, in its true sense, is an entirely voluntary act; it is my response to the needs, expressed or unexpressed, of another human being."[7] As such, response to the Other is an expression of humility. However, there is no spiritual quest for love and philosophical quest for wisdom without epistemic humility. We can find in Gandhi the cultivation of humility which is

6 *Comparative Approaches to Compassion*

accompanied with the acceptance of one's own imperfections. This is actually a move toward the recognition of shared values and the practice of a pluralist and nonviolent form of social interaction and moral interconnectedness. Put differently, humility translates into nonviolent interculturality on a global scale, which cannot be thought of in terms of cultural relativism, but rather as a new mode of projecting and imagining, ethically and politically, a pluralist perspective. Once again, here, the development of humility and the absence of self-centeredness (both at the level of the individuals and nations) require transcending the handicap of ontological fragility which prevents the subject from an active love for the otherness of the Other.

It is hardly necessary to stress the fact that there is no wisdom without love. If philosophy presents itself as a love of wisdom (*philo-sophia*), it is because there is no thinking the world without loving life. To this Thomas Merton adds, "Once we love, our love can change our thinking. But wrong thinking can inhibit love."[8] Merton analyzes the general absence of love in our world because of the existence of a form of meaninglessness which listens and hears no more to the message of those who are inspired by love. And, of course, Merton turns toward Gandhi and his grammar of nonviolence, which he describes as a "devotion to the common good, including that of the adversary."[9] Undoubtedly, the road to wisdom cannot coexist with violence. Therefore, it is clear that the capacity to love depends on one's ability to emerge from violence of fragility as a form of fear of the Other. But while there is insistence on the inherent fragility of human existence and the frailty of the human political condition, one should not forget to point out to the commitment of nonviolence to the dignity of the Other. To respect the dignity of the Other translates into having faith in

Introduction 7

other person's ability to change. As Seneca said: "*Homo sacra res homini*"[10] (Man's life is sacred to man). Man is not God and yet it is sacred. It is sacred because it is its own cause. Man speaks and acts, and through speech and action it creates and destructs. Therefore, Man acts humanly, but always for or against humanity. One way or another, Man invents itself by making history. However, as Lord Byron adds, "History, with all her volumes vast, hath but one page,"[11] and that is freedom. Freedom is not a belief; it is a will. It is a struggle through which *homo fragilis* reinvents themselves. As such, humanism is a fragile adventure, but it is a moral choice for humankind to emphasize its integrity, dignity, and liberty. As Kant puts it, to be wise is to have the ability to be free; that is, to correspond one's action with the principle inherent in the pure practical reason. This said, one can agree with Schopenhauer that what is at the center of moral philosophy is not the question of the "categorical imperative," as Kant says, but the feeling of compassion, which is supposed to arise from metaphysical insight into the unity of humankind.

If we agree with Schopenhauer that the most important feature of *homo fragilis* is suffering, then we can say that compassion or sharing the suffering of the Other is the real basis of human morality. The German word by Schopenhauer to describe compassion is *Mitleid*, which can be translated as "suffering with." According to Schopenhauer, "Only this compassion is the actual basis of all free justice and all genuine loving kindness. Only insofar as an action has originated from compassion does it have moral worth, and anything proceeding from any other motives has none."[12] From a Schopenhauerian perspective, moral agency should inevitably be tied to the subject's capacity to act out of compassion. To act out of compassion is not to suffer in and of oneself, but to share the suffering of the Other. In other words, the Other cannot clearly be distinguished from oneself, since one feels compassion for it. Here we have an effort to overcome indifference and detachment, as the fulfillment of an action toward affinity, empathy, and interconnectedness. Therefore, the capacity to feel concerned with the suffering of the Other is to an expression of aliveness. Compassion is the active concern for life, since the meaning of life is in being connected with the principle of life itself, which is interconnectedness, mutuality, and communion. This means that compassion depends on the absence of narcissism, egoism, and arrogance. In this context, compassion needs a movement toward identification with the person who is compassionate. As Schopenhauer underlines, this is the only way that we can talk about "moral worth" of an action. He observes, "when the ultimate motivating ground for an action or omission lies directly and exclusively in the well being and woe of some other person [...and] intends nothing but that this other remain unharmed or even receive help, support, and relief. This end alone presses the stamp of moral worth on his action or omission."[13] That is to say, one needs to transcend one's well-being in order to be able to identify with the otherness of the Other. "This, however, necessarily presupposes," adds Schopenhauer,

> that I suffer along with his woe, feel his woe, as otherwise I would only mine, and therefore, I immediately will his well being as, otherwise, I would only my own. However, this requires that I be identified with him in some way, i.e., that the complete distinction between me and the other, upon precisely which my egoism rests, to a certain degree be suspended.[14]

It goes without saying that for Schopenhauer compassion or concern about the suffering of the Other is considered as a virtue.

Introduction 9

Nietzsche, however, goes against Schopenhauerian ethics of compassion and rejects the idea of an un-egoistic attachment to the Other. "Nietzsche's concern is that for Schopenhauer, what is shared is general suffering itself, void of particularity, never embedded in a life. If it is only this that we can share, Nietzsche suggests, then we share nothing, and we are never able to affirm particular lives, interests, and pursuits as valuable in themselves."[15] Though Schopenhauer considers Man as an egoistic animal, he leaves the door open to "the everyday phenomenon of *compassion*."[16] Without this virtue of compassion, there could be no sense of solidarity with other human beings. This is a reminder of what Albert Camus affirms in an article written in 1948. "The world I live in is loathsome to me," he underlines, "but I feel one with the men who suffer in it."[17] For Camus, as for many other European writers and intellectuals of his generation, solidarity is a way to confront the horrors of the world and the unhappiness of human beings. As he argues, in his famous lecture at Columbia University in 1946. "It is because the world is unhappy in its essence, that we must do something for happiness, it is because the world is unjust, that we will have to work for justice."[18] Following the argument of Camus, we can say that since Man can never escape its fragility, it has to respond to its common misery through a commitment to compassion. This plea against compassion could be considered as an act of rebellion against the absolutization of fragility in humankind. So, maybe it is time to understand that the maximum fragility in Man implies the maximum compassion.

One cannot avoid tackling the concept of compassion in our world today, where humankind has become so fragile in its confrontation with the problem of violence. Violence has become the indispensable condition for the choice of compassion as the highest moral experience of our existence. That is why there can be no ethical understanding of a human community without any reference to the generating values of love and compassion. As His Holiness the Dalai Lama underscores, "Love and compassion are necessities, not luxuries. Without them, humanity cannot survive."[19] In studying Man of compassion (*miserator hominem*) we shall have to say, each time, whether *homo fragilis* remains faithful to its noble moral promise or it forgets its original purpose as a "being toward love" and plunges back into serving its well-being and success.

"There is solidarity of all men in error and aberration," writes Albert Camus, "and if justice has any meaning in this world, it means nothing but the recognition of that solidarity; it cannot, by its very essence, divorce itself from compassion."[20] If we agree to define humankind as an animal with values, then, we can say that the greatest humanist value in Man is compassion. However, it should be remembered, as Milton says, that Man prefers "to reign in Hell, than serve in Heaven."[21] The fact is that Man can be mean and petty and shallow; a being who sadly overrates itself and tries to expose its ego at any price. But let us not forget that, despite its vice and wickedness, Man can be kind, tender, compassionate, and considerate. Consequently, compassion is a revolution of values in humankind, since Man, as Hegel argues, is a "sick animal." The French radical philosopher, Louis Althusser points out:

> Hegel saw in man a sick animal who neither dies nor recovers (*cet animal malade qui ne meurt ni ne guérit*), but stubbornly insists on living on in a nature terrified of him (*mais s'entête à vivre dans une nature effarée*). The animal kingdom reabsorbs its monsters, the economy its crises: man alone is a triumphant error who makes his aberration the law of the world.[22]

Introduction 11

As such, we can say that Man invented "compassion" in order to fight the evil which is the result of its aberration. Compassion is this nucleus of love which is concealed in the depths of Man's soul. Thanks to this, Man finds itself gravitating in the direction of the suffering Other. In his *Rhetoric*, Aristotle distinguishes acute pity from compassion (*eleos*). Aristotle characterized pity as the excessive form of the medial emotion virtue of compassion. He accordingly rejected it as morally unworthy, for "one who is distressed at undeserved misfortune [i.e., feels compassion] will take pleasure or be unmoved by misfortunes of the opposite sort [i.e., deserved]."[23] Reading Aristotle we can better understand the moderns and their conception of "compassion." Nobody explains better the Aristotelian point of view on compassion than Rousseau, when he affirms: "we are attached to our fellows less by the sentiment of their pleasures than by the sentiment of their pains."[24]

Among the moderns, Descartes has an interesting point of view on compassion, since for him, the compassionate love is not a form of desire, but the thought of something which is beneficent. In that case, "Love, inasmuch as it is the thought that something is good, gathers its force from reason which ultimately determines good. As such, perfect love preserves an intellectual nature: it is not so much passion as action."[25] Descartes in *Les Passions de l'âme* (*Passions of the Soul*) analyzes in depth the concept of compassion. According to him, the evil that happens to others arouses compassion. But compassion is not necessarily pity. For Descartes, "Pity is a kind of sadness mingled with love or with good will towards those whom we see suffering some misfortune that we think they don't deserve."[26] As for compassion, it is a concern for the Other which supposes a detachment of the subject in relation to his own good. Therefore, the consideration of the interest of the Other is correlative to a detachment from one's own interest. Compassion is the ideal of a passionate life accompanied by a well-founded self-esteem, that is to say, a life in which love takes precedence over desire. The compassionate man is never fearful of the other person, because it is not envious of other person's possessions and is satisfied with what it has. Compassion is the ideal of a social life accompanied by a well-founded self-esteem. That is to say, it is a life in which friendly love takes precedence over sexual or romantic desire. As such, the compassionate man is never fearful of the other person, because it is not envious of other person's possessions and is satisfied with what it has. In the final analysis, compassionate love is placed by Descartes in the soul, in accord with right reason. As such, with Descartes, compassionate love preserves an intellectual nature. According to Descartes:

> Love is a commotion of the soul caused by a movement of the spirits, a commotion that impels the soul to join itself *de volonté* to objects that appear to be agreeable to it. And hatred is a spirit-caused commotion impelling the soul to want to be separated from objects that appear to be harmful. In saying that these commotions are caused by the spirits, I am distinguishing love and hatred—which are passions, and depend on the body—from judgments that also bring the soul to join itself *de volonté* to things it deems good and to separate itself from ones that it deems bad, and also from the commotions that these judgments, with no help from the body, produce in the soul.[27]

Descartes expresses no ambivalence toward the work and action of the soul in relation with the question of compassion. He considers compassion as a moral response to others, in which our own worth and the worth of the Other go hand in hand.

While Descartes's economical definition of compassion is intellectual, with Spinoza, compassion, like any other virtue, is celebrated as an "extended self" contributing to social harmony. Spinoza "repeatedly extols the benefit of living among other rational individuals. The more that we live under the sway of reason, the more we will understand the benefit of social harmony, and will desire that same good for others. Hence preservation of the self will include preservation of social order and justice. The 'self' of self-preservation refers not only to the individual, but also to those with whom, broadly speaking, he or she has a relationship of mutual benefit."[28] Spinoza uses the concept of "nobility" (*generositas*) as a form of love practiced in return of the other person's hatred. In fact, Spinoza explains nobility as "the desire whereby every individual, according to the dictates of reason alone, endeavors to assist others and make friends of them."[29] In other words, nobility is a selfless action which is directed to the benefit of the Other. Compassion is also an active and noble emotion, which rejoices at another's happiness and suffers from another's pain.

As it is based on love, compassion does not imply distance from the suffering individual. The suffering individual is someone with whom we have associated pleasure, so an emotional bond already exists between us. Although pain is an aspect of compassion, as much as it is of pity, we do not hold ourselves apart from a suffering friend. Compassion is a much deeper emotion than pity; it implies a certain equality between the parties involved, and the fact that a friend's suffering will not adversely affect our opinion of her.[30]

Compassion is, therefore, linked to a morally strong aspect of human life, since it contributes to the emotional growth of the individual and the society.

14   *Comparative Approaches to Compassion*

We can find the same morally positive experience of the self in Montaigne's attitude toward compassion. As he announces in the opening essay of the first volume of his *Essais*, "I am much inclined to mercie, and affected to mildnesse. So it is, that in mine opinion, I should more naturally stoope unto compassion, than bend to estimation. Yet is pitty held a vicious passion among the Stoicks. They would have us aid the afflicted, but not to faint, and co- suffer with them."[31] No one better than Shakespeare understood the value of compassion. In his play *Coriolanus*, he shows the legendary fifth-century BC general by the same name, who is banished by his native city, when he remembers how to weep and proclaims: "It is no small thing to make mine eyes sweat compassion."[32] Compassion is also an emotional attitude which is identified by Shakespeare in his famous play *The Tempest*. In the famous speech by Prospero in the epilogue of this play, compassion is given a final voice. "Let me not," Prospero says to us:

Since I have my dukedom got,
And pardoned the deceiver, dwell
In this bare island by your spell,
But release me from my bands
With the help of your good hands.
Gentle breath of yours my sails
Must fill, or else my project fails,
Which was to please. Now I want
Spirits to enforce, art to enchant;
And my ending is despair
Unless I be relieved by prayer,
Which pierces so that it assaults
Mercy itself, and frees all faults.
As you from crimes would pardoned be,
Let your indulgence set me free.[33]

Introduction 15

Shakespeare does not consider compassion as a simple passion of the soul. It is certainly for him a moral choice. As such we can say that compassion is a concept which is situated at the heart of Shakespeare humanist view of Man. "Even in his villains, Shakespeare generally finds something to admire, some saving grace, some extenuating circumstance. No man is altogether a lost soul for him."[34] Shakespeare portrays Romans in his tragedies as men of violence, vengeance, and reprisal. However, Shakespeare does not hate the Romans and his cloudless humanist view embraces not a bloodthirsty character like Titus Andronicus, but it certainly applies to a Stoic mind like Seneca, as a philosopher of mercy and compassion, rather than pity, which he considered as "a vice of the mind [*vitium animi*]."[35]

It has been a commonplace to regard Stoic's account of compassion and sympathy as an important contribution to the debates on moral evaluation of the Other and the sentiment of humanity. According to the Oxford philosopher, Sir Richard Sorabji, the Stoic concept of *oikeiosis* reflects the idea of human attachment to the Other, including the whole human family.[36] Stoics considered *oikeiosis* as a mental and emotional attitude of concern for the Other. The Stoic account of *oikeiosis* and moral development provides us with a self-awareness that Man is an animal who confers values on things, such as freedom and justice. Here is where the idea of sharing and association with others takes root among the Stoic philosophers and those influenced by it. Cicero explains this sphere of sharing as what he calls "a community of human association." He argues the following:

In the whole of morality… there is nothing more brilliant, nor of greater extent than the association of people with other people, a kind of community and sharing of advantages and

16 *Comparative Approaches to Compassion*

a real affection for the human race. It is born with us from conception, since children are loved by their parents, and the whole household is held together by marriage and offspring, and gradually spreads abroad, first through kin relationships, then marriage connections, then friendships, then relations of proximity, then to fellow-citizens and those who are allies and friends politically, and finally embraces the entire race. This attitude of the mind, which allots to each their own, and maintains this community of human association... is called justice.[37]

As we can observe, Cicero is a classical thinker who recognizes the necessity of friendship and affection for the Other in human existence. Undoubtedly, when it comes to Cicero's influence on Christian thinkers like Augustine and Aquinas, there is a great deal to say about the philosophical affinities of Stoicism and Christianity. Consequently, there are many elements of Stoic ethics which are helpful to understand more fully the Christian approach to the concept of compassion. Let us not forget that "the Roman Stoics, particularly Seneca, were influential among the Church Fathers starting in the second century and continuing through the middle ages. John Calvin also built upon insights of the Roman Stoics. Many of these Christian adaptations of Stoicism drew heavily from ethical writings."[38] However, one should also not underestimate the role of Oriental religions like Hinduism and Buddhism in the spiritual and philosophical evolution of the concept of compassion in the Western canon. If a core tenet of Buddhist ethics is compassion, then *ahimsa* is considered by the Buddhists as an ethical imperative in thought and in action. This requires understanding how compassion and nonviolence provide the moral and political guidelines to construct a better society. It goes without saying that the theorists and practitioners of nonviolence in history were fully aware of the fact that they had to choose to live by their ethical principles and to be mindfully conscious of the nonviolent consequences of their intentions, speech, and actions. The term *nonviolence*, of course, can be used in a variety of ways ranging from moral dissent to Gandhian *Satyagraha* and civil disobedience. But here, we have in mind to show that nonviolence is the power of compassion, or to say it more directly nonviolence is an active expression of the social and political engagement of compassion. The moral nature of compassion lies firstly in the simple principle of honoring the dignity of the Other. Compassion is morally superior to any other human act precisely because of its willingness to protect the otherness of the Other. The power of compassion addresses the human wrongs without resorting to wrong means. Compassion, also, provides a way to engage or perhaps even inhabit the otherness of the Other without using physical or mental violence. In fact, as the next few chapters will show us, compassion is an element of deep mutual understanding which can be a nonviolent driver of social and political change. Perhaps, with such a universal appeal and with inherent moral qualities, compassion is the expression of a fundamental commitment to nonviolence and the pursuit of peace in today's world.

Compassion is the only virtue in *homo fragilis* which is accompanied with a sense of wholeness and interconnectedness. Deprived of its harmonious compassionate roots, *homo fragilis* would be confronted permanently by the presence of evil in history and horrified to discover by the great number of its failures and crimes against the living beings. As such, what the following pages will show us is that without compassion *homo fragilis* has always been deprived of spiritual direction. But whenever and wherever *homo fragilis* has been guided by compassion to humanity and sensibility, the very challenges of human history have found their answers in the nonviolent spirituality of humankind. Truly, *homo fragilis* as a spiritual witness of its own history has tried to confront with love and compassion the violence present at the tail of its historical existence. And yet, compassion has always been a fragile blossom of *homo fragilis*. Curiously, compassion is born out of an ill-designed world by a fragile living being. Maybe, that is why nonviolence is an awareness of the world, a particular way of relating to the history of spirituality and that of life with compassion. This history unites humanity with the bonds of empathetic fellowship, universal love, and nonviolence. After all, compassion is the spirit of harmony in which all hearts and minds of human history have worked and moved. After all, civilization is a creation of human compassion, a shrine which cannot be reached without making the pilgrimage.

1

Ahimsa in Jainism, Buddhism, and Hinduism: A Compassionate View of Life

Ahimsa is a Sanskrit word derived from the root (*hiṃsā*) which means to harm or to strike. *Ahimsa* refers specifically to the opposite of violence and hurting. In today's world, we refer to the concept of *ahimsa* to describe a moral or spiritual attitude of harmlessness, non-killing, and nonviolence. *Ahimsa* is the key concept of the three religions that originated in ancient India: Hinduism, Buddhism, and Jainism. It is hardly necessary to point out that there is a basic identity in the broad conception of non-killing among the Buddhist, the Jain, and the Hindu doctrines. As such, compassion for the other living beings and the total avoidance of violence are necessary to ascetic life in these three religions. However:

> In ancient India, *ahimsa* was an instrument/agency of action rather than the real action itself, and one did not encounter the development of an autonomous and full-scale philosophy of *ahimsa* in early India, but as appendages of larger philosophies. Even in Buddhism, *ahimsa* was part of *sheel* (conduct), and enjoyed a lower status in comparison to *karuna* (compassion) and *maitreyi.* (love, benevolence).[1]

As a result, we can see here the compassionate attitude toward life and the emergence of emphasis on *ahimsa* as part of a worldview which considers the practice of self-restraint and nonviolence as modes of action related to the metaphysical acceptance of the sameness of life. For example, in the Vedic tradition what makes the doctrine of *ahimsa* the key to the idea of a compassionate attitude in life is certainly the belief in an ultimate metaphysical realization of the absolute and faultless sameness of Brahman in one chain of Being. A similar view of the matter may be discerned in Buddhism and Jainism, though one needs to take into consideration the essential differences between Hinduism and the other two religions. Nonetheless, if life has any value for these three religious doctrines, it has value only in relation with the concept of *ahimsa*. *Ahimsa*, therefore, is a key concept in Hindu, Jain, and Buddhist traditions which is understood as an exemplary individual abstention from direct himsa. In other words, we are not talking here about the Gandhian use of this term as involving truth (satya) and self-sacrifice. However, it is important to note that Gandhi's use of the concept of *ahimsa* is directly related to the influence of Jainism and his Jain mentor Shrimad Rajchandra (1867–1901).

Consequently, any conceptual history of the word *ahimsa* should start with a survey of Jainism. Jainism is part of the great spiritual movements in Indian thought during the post-Vedic period. In this respect, Jainism is a religious tradition that is contemporary with Buddhism. In fact, Jainism opposed, in the manner of Buddhism, the corruption that was afflicting Hinduism by questioning practices such as the caste system. During the fifth century BCE Siddhartha Gautama, the founder of Buddhism, who later became known as the Buddha announced his doctrine of the Four Noble Truths (*Chatvari-arya-satyani*), emphasizing the truth of suffering, the truth of the cause of suffering, the truth of the end of suffering, and the truth of the path that initiates the end of suffering. Almost at the same time, the sage Vardhamana later given the title Mahavira (the great hero), introduced the method of sense control by means of gradual deprivation and set an example by his conduct. He left his home at the age of thirty and wandered for twelve years in search of salvation. However, at the age of forty-two he attained enlightenment and founded an order of naked priests and taught his doctrine for thirty years. He died in 468 BC at the age of seventy-two in the Patna region. Jainism takes its name from the doctrine expounded by a *jina*, an individual who attained supreme knowledge by mastering his earthly steps. By conquering control of his five senses and turning away all its *karmas*, the *jina* attains supreme knowledge and spends the rest of his life in *Dharma Prabhavana*, preaching the principles of the Jain religion to human beings. It is because of this noble task that a *jina* is also called a *Tirthankara*, i.e., one who helps human beings cross the ocean of life by providing them with a boat in the form of *Dharma* (law or duty). According to the first principle of Jainism, human being is a dual creature: it is both material and spiritual. It is not a perfect being, because its soul (*jiva*) undergoes the place imposed by *karma*. So it goes through various incarnations, going through the circle of rebirths (*samsara*), sometimes in a higher form, sometimes in a lower form. When matter exerts its full influence, *karma* has its full effect. The universe, according to Jainism, is divided between the soul (*jiva*) and the non-soul or inanimate substance (*ajiva*). The entire Jain philosophy is based on the interaction of these two principles. It is the interaction between all that is living and all that is non-living that produces the elements of life such as birth and death. Five inanimate substances are opposed to the soul: matter, space (*akasa*), time (*kala*), the cause of movement (*dharma*) and the cause of rest (*adharma*). Thus the general conditions of being

22   *Comparative Approaches to Compassion*

are defined. But how does matter attach itself to the soul? *Karma*, which is of a material nature, attaches itself to the soul by an influx, or *asrava*, and imposes on it a place (*bandha*) by subjecting it to successive rebirths (*samsara*). In order for the soul to free itself from matter, the moral law must show it the means.

The principles of Jain morality are contained in the five prescriptions or commandments called "*vartas.*" They must be respected and applied in all circumstances. The first of these prohibitions is the strict duty of *ahimsa* (non-harm). For Jains, compassion, as not harming the Other, is the supreme law. A Jain monk must refrain from killing any living thing. To injure, cause pain, or destroy living beings is considered the most serious sin. Jain sutras such as *Acharanga Sutra* and *Sutrakritanga Sutra* present non-compassion and harm (*himsa*) as the major sin on every page. According to Jainism, what creates violence is not only the harmful act, but more importantly the intention to harm and the absence of compassion. That is why *ahimsa* is not a negative state of mind. It is the expression of a positive virtue which is compassion. As such, for Jainism, *ahimsa* enfolds unity of compassion as intention and the action of nonviolence. Therefore, it demands respect and responsibility for every life form. As a result, according to the precepts of Jainism, a man cannot practice *ahimsa* and be non-compassionate. Indeed, "Basing itself on *Anckantavada*, a metaphysical view that Reality is many-faceted, Jainism has championed the cause of *ahimsa* in full vigour, not only by openly condemning wanton cruelty to any creature, but by making it mandatory in practice to avoid harming any kind of living creatures to the extent that is humanly possible."[2] But though a metaphysical doctrine, Jainism remains also very pragmatic. As such, the compassionate approach of Jainism to life

Ahimsa *in Jainism, Buddhism, and Hinduism*

and living beings in general demands a full application of *ahimsa* in relation to the economic, social, and political enterprises of human beings. "Such an encompassing meaning of *ahimsa* envisions global harmony consisting of man and nature. In case of man, *ahimsa* encapsulates unity of action and intention while in case of nature it demands respect for every life form."[3] In some respect, a*himsa* and Jainism stand as parallel terms. Not only are they parallel but are also so interconnected that one is incomplete without the other. Maybe that is the reason why Mahatma Gandhi was so directly inspired by the concept of *ahimsa* in Jainism that he revitalized it under the name of "nonviolence" and took it into account in a broader context of global politics.

As it was pointed out, Jain monk's compassion and respect for life extends to all its forms, whether it be human, animal, plant, water, or even fire. But, according to the principles of Jainism, showing compassion toward all that lives is not enough; one must also abstain from lying and renounce all forms of property. *Ahimsa* is therefore practiced by the Jain monk in a form of activity that is at once corporal, mental, and verbal. *Ahimsa* is the supreme law (ahimsa paramo dharma) and the ultimate ideal of the Jain monk is self-realization. There are many similarities between Buddhism and Jainism when it comes to understanding the essential role of *ahimsa* in these two religious doctrines. Actually, they both emphasize on *dharma* (moral duty) and *moksa* (liberation) and *ahimsa* (nonviolence). Consequently:

> Buddhist thought attempted to give *ahimsa* a wider significance by forbidding all forms of *himsa*, or injury to sentient beings, and by encouraging a constant effort to remove the suffering of others, as expressed in the idea of *karuna*, or compassion. What is truly remarkable is the way these philosophers link

24   *Comparative Approaches to Compassion*

the cognitive, the volitional and the emotional aspects of their enquiry into values.[4]

In the Buddhist doctrine, pain and suffering give meaning to the concept of compassion. It is because all life is pain and suffering that human beings should be compassionate and nonviolent. The human being suffers because it is dependent on its "Self." Therefore, at the origin of pain is the desire for the "Self." It is actually an attachment to the world, which constitutes the force of *Karma*, that is not affected by death. According to the teachings of the Buddha, desire must be suppressed in order to put an end to pain and the cycle of rebirths. Buddhism, therefore, suggests a complete destruction of all thought of the Self, which opens the door to *Nirvana*, a state defined by the extinction of passions. As such, human beings must purify themselves of all selfishness and of all sins, by defying all forms of pleasure and desire. Interestingly, Buddhism considers hatred and anger as forms of desire. Anger in the mind gives rise to anger in the act. So, in order to follow the path of wisdom, humans must have a just thought. To be unjust, according to the Buddha, is to be uncompassionate and violent. In other words, in the Buddhist philosophy, justice and *ahimsa* go hand in hand. As a result, *ahimsa* is the highest of virtues, because the Bodhisattva is an ocean of compassion and tolerance. Buddhism proclaims compassion for the enemies and non-harm for all living beings. As it is said in *The Dhammapada*: "Not to commit any sin, to do good, and to purify one's mind, that is the teaching of (all) the Awakened."[5] Thus, what Buddhism teaches is that there can be no peace of mind against hardship and suffering in life with compassion. And, this is not only for the good of others but also for the happiness of oneself. As His Holiness the Dalai Lama, who is believed by Tibetan Buddhists to be the manifestation of the Bodhisattva of Compassion, underlines:

> The first beneficiary of compassion is always oneself. When compassion, or warmheartedness, arises in us and shifts our focus away from our own narrow self-interest, it is as if we open an inner door. Compassion reduces our fear, boosts our confidence, and brings us a sense of connection with them and a sense of purpose and meaning in life. Compassion also gives us respite from our own difficulties.[6]

What can be concluded from Dalai Lama's comments on compassion is that Buddhism by modifying the preexisting Vedic concept of *ahimsa* recognized that the intentional harming of some life carried deep moral consequences.

> Buddhism, however, never took the concept of *ahimsa* to the logical extreme of Jainism. The Buddha criticized the Vedic Brahmans concerning animal sacrifice but did not forbid livelihoods that entailed the unintentional taking of life such as farming. Along with Jainism and Hinduism, Buddhism discouraged livelihoods such as fishing, hunting, or butchering and also held to vegetarianism as logical outcomes of *ahimsa*. It would seem that although the overriding principle is that of *ahimsa*, Buddhism recognizes that one cannot follow this principle absolutely, that day-to-day living entails some unintentional and largely unavoidable taking of some sentient life.[7]

To be sure, one cannot understand Mahayana Buddhism without the radical form of compassion as an altruistic behavior combined with *ahimsa*. Here, the concept of "suffering with" is as important as "non-harming" the Other. As such, in the context of Mahayana

Buddhism, compassion demands much more than just sweet talk. As a matter of fact, compassion is a very serious moral imperative which connotes kindness, generosity, and responsibility.

> Compassion, according to the Dalai Lama, is an attitude that not only wishes for others to be free of their suffering, but is also "associated with a sense of commitment, responsibility, and respect towards the other." He insists that the commitment, responsibility, and respect engendered by compassion impel us to help others if we can. A compassionate person isn't one who merely renders lip service to freeing others from suffering or one who expresses a vague wish that others be happy. Instead, the Dalai Lama says that a compassionate person develops a strong commitment to free others from suffering and its causes and to experience happiness.[8]

His Holiness the Dalai Lama, therefore, makes a connection between the compassionate intention and act of the Self and the unhappiness of the Other. There is at this point an inseparable relationship between the emotional and the moral on the one hand and the absence of self-interest in relation with the care for the otherness of the Other on the other. As we can see, the ethic of compassion is the key element of nonviolent action and exercise of justice in Tibetan Buddhism. This is a subject which is at the heart of the teachings of His Holiness the Dalai Lama. According to him:

> Nothing in the principle of compassion—the wish to see others relieved of suffering—involves surrendering to the misdeeds of others. Nor does compassion demand that we meekly accept injustice. Far from promoting weakness or passivity, compassion requires great fortitude and strength of character. Some of the great fighters against injustice of recent times, people of strong character and determination like Mahatma Gandhi, Mother

Teresa, Nelson Mandela, Martin Luther King, Jr., Vaclav Havel and others-have been motivated by universal compassion. One could not describe such people as meek or retiring just because they combined their devotion to the welfare of others with a commitment to nonviolence.[9]

In other words, when it comes to injustice and wrongdoing, Buddhism (in the same way as Jainism and Hinduism) turns to the two concepts of compassion and *ahimsa* to restore the balance in life.

Compassion is the kind of virtue that can be extended limitlessly. Unlike material goods, compassion can't be exhausted. Tibetan Buddhism observes that as compassion increases in its scope or breadth, it also increases its depth. The person who practices compassion can feel the same depth of love, the same intimacy, for all sentient beings that he or she feels toward family and close friends. Compassion makes us feel connected to sentient individuals in a way that transforms us.[10]

Consequently, the search for justice in Tibetan Buddhism, and more specifically in the philosophy of the Dalai Lama extends the concept of compassion to what Mario Aguilar calls "a communal identity of a shared humanity." As he explains in his book *The 14th Dalai Lama: Peacekeeping and Universal Responsibility*:

A communal identity of a shared humanity arises out of a text that reflects the developments of Tibetan Buddhism not as an individual philosophy but as a socio-communal way of life in which the acquiring of *bodhicitta* aims at the formation of a *bodhisattva* who instead of leaving the cycle of suffering remains within such cycle in order to aid others in need. Identity then becomes not an individual trace but a communal one dictating laws of human interaction, nature and metaphysics that provide

28   *Comparative Approaches to Compassion*

for the relatedness of human beings and sentient beings. Identity then depends on a shared humanity while a shared humanity depends on a *bodhisattva*.[11]

If we turn to Hinduism, we can observe clearly that the idea of shared humanity as the compassionate accommodation of the "Self" and the "Other" is present in the *Bhagavad-Gita*, the most revered book in the Hindu culture. We can also find the *Bhagavad-Gita* at the center of many philosophical and religious debates in the West. Though the *Bhagavad-Gita* influenced many great figures of the nineteenth-century European thought, such as Leo Tolstoy, Arthur Schopenhauer and Henry David Thoreau, but its most famous and pertinent reader has been none other than Mahatma Gandhi. For Gandhi, the message of the *Gita* is that of *ahimsa* and compassion based on selfless action. Gandhi understood perfectly the tension between renunciation and action in the *Gita*.

> In his interpretation of the *Gita*, Gandhi refers to the battlefield of Kurukshetra as the heart of man in which the two natures of selfishness and unselfishness are engaged in combat. The great need, in his view, is to cultivate selfless or detached action to the exclusion of egocentric activity. This is made possible for us by means of sacrifice, devotion and the service of others. Through the disciplines of such action, that is, through karma yoga, which involves *ahimsa*, we come to the realization of Truth or God, for to realize God is to see Him in all that lives, and to recognize our oneness with all creation.[12]

The Gandhian approach to the *Gita* is the correct way of addressing the question of compassion in this book and in Hinduism. The reader is invited to meditate on the dialectic of the self-knowledge and self-sacrifice. As a result, the warrior is invited to control his passions and become a disciplined person. The *Gita* is therefore presented as a search for the self through devotion. At every stage of the book, Krishna is aware of the spiritual conflict that is tearing Arjuna's soul, and he guides him to the appropriate path, so that he can resolve his internal tensions. Krishna invites him not to kill but to renounce his attachment to the fruits of action. As a result of this lesson, Arjuna learns to control his action and emotions without leaving the scene of the battle. As a result, the *Gita* is an expression of the Hindu preoccupation with the ethical in a context of praxis and pragmatism. Ethical action is valued by the *Gita* because it makes possible the fullest development of the human agency. While correcting predominantly the elitism of the Vedas and the Upanishads, the *Gita* suggests that the way of happiness should be in accordance with dharma and beyond all forms of selfishness as the culmination of ethical life. Consistent with this stand, the *Gita* remains explicitly assertive on justice and equality, opening the door to the lower castes, including the illiterate. As Max Weber argues in his famous "The Profession and Vocation of Politics":

> Hinduism was therefore able to elaborate the *dharma* for each caste, from the ascetics and Brahmins down to the rogues and whores, according to the immanent and particular laws governing each occupation, including war and politics. How war is fitted in fitted into the totality of the orders of life can be found in the *Bhagavad Gita*, in the discussion between Krishna and Arjuna. "Do what is necessary", which means whatever "work" is imposed as a duty by the *dharma* of the warrior caste and its rules, whatever is objectively necessary in relation to the purpose of war. According to this belief, acting thus is not injurious to religious salvation; indeed it serves this end.[13]

By reading these lines from Max Weber, we can understand that he was well aware of the *Gita*'s contribution to the ethics of duty, truthfulness, and compassion in Indian philosophical and spiritual traditions. The background of war in the *Gita* is nothing but a metaphor to confront human beings with the qualities that can make them either demon-like or divine. Accordingly, the *Gita* advocates all the positive virtues which are also important to Jainism and Buddhism, such as: forgiveness, humility, absence of hatred, compassion, and nonviolence. Therefore, in Hinduism *ahimsa* and compassion, next to duty and righteousness, are pre-requisites for any spiritual progress. In all and for all, the spiritual being needs to integrate the sense of self-control and recognition of the similarity of self and the other with a perception of the sameness of life and non-hatred and non-harm of all souls.

In a nutshell, from the point of view of a compassionate and nonviolent eye, none of the three philosophical religions of India are individualistic doctrines. As such, their metaphysical principles and moral precepts do not concern solely an individual isolated from its fellow humans. Nor are they concerned with the *Moksha* (liberation from the cycle of death and rebirth) or *Nirvana* (the blowing out and the end of suffering) of an individual divorced from all life's activities. On the contrary, though the practices and dogmas differ in these three religions, the principles of compassion and *ahimsa* are the same. Mahatma Gandhi was well aware of this fact when he said that "true religion and true morality are inseparably bound up with each other."[14] According to him, as long as human beings could reach the heart of this morality, i.e., *ahimsa* and compassion, they could reach the heart of all the religions. Gandhi's equation of compassion and *ahimsa*, which Buddhism, Hinduism, and Jainism share, also implies that the concept of compassion "has no geographical limits."[15] But it is not just the religious fraternity of Indian religions that is brought here to the fore by Gandhi, but the unitary nature of compassion which, according to him, transcends all religions. When we turn to Gandhi, as a true fellow traveler and accomplice of Indian and non-Indian religions, we understand that for a thinker and practitioner of nonviolence like him, there is a direct line which links the *Bhagavad-Gita* to the *Sermon on the Mount* of Jesus Christ. Hence he argued transparently, "Supposing a Christian came to me and said he was captivated by the reading of *Bhagavat* and so wanted to declare himself a Hindu," I should say to him: "No. What *Bhagavat* offers, the Bible also offers. You have not made the attempt to find it out. Make the attempt and be a good Christian."[16] Gandhi, most probably, had no idea that one day his dream of a compassionate world with a possible dialogue among faiths would be that of an African-American Baptist minister and civil rights activist by the name of Martin Luther King, Jr. However, Gandhi had a deep conviction in the Christian approach to the concepts of love and compassion. He knew well that, as in the case of Hinduism, Buddhism, and Jainism, Christian compassionate love was a mode of thinking and a way of life which would help the oppressed people to struggle for freedom, while transforming the moral disposition of their adversary. As for the Indian religions, the Christian ethic of compassion challenges us with new urgency.

2

Love and Compassion in Christianity:
From Jesus Christ to Thomas Merton

The Jain, Buddhist, and Hindu belief in compassion is handsomely summed up in the first epistle of John: "Let us love one another; for love is God and everyone that loves is born of God and knows God."[1] Throughout the history of Christianity, Christian philosophers and saints have variously involved themselves with the concept of "compassion." More often than not, they preferred to talk about "mercy," rather than compassion. However, the Greek word used in the *New Testament* is the noun *éleos* (ἔλεος) which could be translated as either "mercy" or "compassion." The *Gospels* mention the adjective *eleēmōn* in reference to Jesus Christ as a person who is merciful and compassionate. In Jesus's *Sermon on the Mount* found in the *Gospel of Matthew* we read: "Fortunate are the merciful, for they shall find mercy!"[2] Jesus calls on his Apostles and followers to look at the oppressed "from below" and with mercy and compassion. So Jesus teaches that compassion is directed, not only toward the miserable and afflicted, but also in relation with a crowd without a shepherd. In the *Gospel of Mark* it is said: "As Jesus went ashore he saw a large crowd, and he had compassion on them for they were like sheep without a shepherd."[3] Amazingly, the words "mercy" or "compassion" are absent in the *Gospel of John*. However, Jesus repeats the famous commandment to his Apostles: "Just as I have loved you, you also must love one another."[4] As we can see, in the *New Testament*, the three concepts of "love," "mercy," and "compassion" are expressed interchangeably. Jesus Christ is the prophet of love and the father of all mercies and compassions. That is why, Jesus also teaches that one should show mercy to others, just as God has mercy on him or her. It is written in the *Gospel of Luke*: "Be merciful, just as your Father is merciful."[5] Jesus speaks to all who believe in him in the language of compassion. In each of his encounters and teachings, compassion occupies a central position and signals a turning point in the event. What the Matthean beatitudes show us is that compassion and humility are closely related in the acts and speeches of Christ. Jesus's humility and peacefulness are signs of his compassionate temperament, and a strong expression of his philosophy of nonviolence. Jesus placed a unique emphasis on the notion of love for the enemy and ethic of empathy and nonviolence.

The *Sermon on the Mount*, as witnessed and described by the *Gospels of Matthew* and *Luke*, is a masterpiece of the literature on compassion and nonviolence. From the first centuries of the Christian era to the present day, Jesus's words on the Mount have provided a rich moral and religious teaching to all those, believers and non-believers alike, who have preached a message of peace, brotherhood, and nonviolence. For Saint Augustine, this sermon of Jesus was the perfect charter of Christian life, while a spiritual pilgrim like Tolstoy saw it as the cornerstone of Christian nonviolence. As such, for more than twenty centuries, Christian philosophers, mystics, and peacemakers saw in the *Sermon on the Mount* the ethical foundations of love, compassion, and social justice. It also provided a philosophical and theological basis for the struggle of great social reformers like Martin Luther King, Jr., Desmond Tutu and Adolfo Pérez Esquivel. As for Gandhi,

Love and Compassion in Christianity 35

who can be considered as the father of nonviolence in modern times, he also referred directly in his writings and speeches to the *Sermon on the Mount* of Jesus Christ. Yet, strange as it may seem, and unlike the general use of the word *ahimsa* in the Jain, Buddhist, and Hindu scriptures, Jesus Christ preaches the idea of nonviolence, without using the word itself. However, it is precisely in the demands of Jesus in his *Sermon* that we can find the idea of nonviolence. The God that is revealed to us by Jesus is a God of nonviolence, and Christ himself exemplifies a nonviolent prophet.

Jesus challenges political violence and social injustice from the very first day of his prophetic commitment. For example, in the *Gospel of Luke*, we see that the reign of God is announced by Jesus as a sovereignty of compassion and mercy. The parable of the two sons in *Luke 15:11-32* reveals the nonviolent gesture of a father who in compassion receives back into the fold his younger son against the indisposition of his elder son.

In this parable, "the father is a figure of God who in his mercy is at work in Jesus among sinners and the righteous. The younger son represents the tax collectors and sinners... while the elder son is a figure of the Pharisees and Scribes... The parable continues the Lukan theme of Jesus as a tension between the outcasts and the righteous in his ministry of extending the pardoning love of God to humanity.(...) The parable underscores in this context the fact that the mercy needed by the son and requested for is the prerogative of only the father who freely exercises it and would ordinarily not be reprimanded for refusing it. It is gratuitous and springs from the very goodness of the heart from which love and kindness flow (...) The parable therefore educates on the need for mercy as an imitation of the love of God and a participation in the compassion of God. God desires mercy for sinners and each time humans offer this mercy and create opportunities for repentance God's will is accomplished."[6]

In the *Gospel of Matthew,* Jesus often appears as an educator preaching wisdom and nonviolent moral law. He is seen as a lawgiver who has come to establish certain laws and to change others. For this reason, the *Sermon on the Mount* includes both beatitudes and sentences, especially those on social justice and love of the enemies. The beatitudes are seen as the proclamation of good news. Jesus proclaims happy all those who are poor and thirsty for justice. He beatifies the poor and the persecuted because they do not oppress anyone. He invites us to be poor, merciful, gentle, and he tells us to thirst for justice. But this choice of nonviolence proposed by Jesus is complemented by a new justice, which includes an overcoming of the previous law. In relation to the old law of Moses, Jesus puts forward his own interpretation of the divine law. He does not set out to reject the law, but to complete it, being himself in his person the fulfillment of the law and the prophets. This section of the *Gospel of Matthew* (5: 14-48) includes the moral imperative of love of the enemies. "You have heard what was said: You shall love your neighbor and may hate your enemy. But I say unto you, love your enemies, do good to them that hate you, pray for them that [mistreat and] persecute you."[7]

Jesus gives a merciful and compassionate character to the precepts of the Old Testament. The nonviolent radicalism of Jesus, thus, affects every human being and not only the Christian. The faithful must become "perfect" as the heavenly Father is perfect. As such, Jesus's commitment to nonviolence goes beyond the teaching of solely a higher ethic. His ethical requirement is marked by an ontological transformation of the believer. He asks

Love and Compassion in Christianity   37

his apostles to commit themselves morally in order to belong to the Kingdom of God. Therefore, the golden rule that sums up the compassionate and nonviolent essence of the *Sermon on the Mount* is this: "Whatever you want men to do to you, do it to them. This is the Law and the prophets."[8] Undoubtedly, the radical requirement that translates the nonviolent message of Jesus is manifested by a certain quality of look at others. By preaching love for the enemy, he refuses to enter into the spiral of violence. He invites everyone to join the vast movement of love of which God himself is the author, and of which Jesus, is the privileged messenger. Thus divine love takes on human form in the deeds and actions of the Galilean, as the philosophical and theological foundation of a nonviolent transformation of the world. Last but not least, one can say that there is a clearly formulated doctrine of nonviolent action in the *Gospels*, but above all Jesus himself can be considered as a radical philosopher and practitioner of nonviolence. This is why remarkable human beings like Saint Francis, Tolstoy, Simone Weil, Gandhi, Martin Luther King, Jr., and Thomas Merton claimed over centuries to have chosen the compassionate and nonviolent path of Jesus against injustice, inequality, and oppression.

Perhaps no one is closer to the compassionate character and nonviolent vision of Jesus Christ than Saint Francis of Assisi. Francis of Assisi can be considered as the man of the return to the teachings of Christ. He is the man of the gospel of poverty and fraternity. He is also the man of the renewal of the *Gospels*. Through his original and nonviolent reading of the *Gospels*, he formulated a new relationship between humankind and the world. As a matter of fact, the true spiritual dimension of Saint Francis's evangelical experience comes precisely from the encounter between the nonviolent message of Jesus and the history of the

Middle Ages in Europe. In the heart of the Italian society of the twelfth century, Francis of Assisi discovered, like all Christian mystics, a new face of God, very different from what was taught by the Church and the Christian sovereigns of his time. Born in 1182 into a wealthy family, Francesco Bernardone was destined to become a merchant like his father, who often crossed the Alps for his business. Cheerful and kind, naturally playful and very sociable, he soon became the darling of the golden girls of the small town of Assisi, spending his time organizing parties and joyful evenings. A poet by temperament, he nevertheless dreamed of becoming a knight and joining the ranks of the papal militia to fight the imperial armies in southern Italy. But he stopped halfway along his route, in Spoleto, where he was challenged by an inner voice that asked him to turn back to his hometown. Back in Assisi, he abandoned his old friends and sought silence and solitude to pray. Disillusioned with the pleasures of his past life, he decided to go on a pilgrimage to Rome to visit the tomb of the Apostles and come face to face with God. In Rome, he mingled with the beggars in the square in front of the Basilica of St. Peter. He approached the miserable and the poor and became more and more attentive to the misery of others. On his return to Assisi, he sold several pieces of scarlet cloth in his father's store to finance the restoration of the oratory of the church of *San Damiano*. Indignant at his son's new lifestyle, Pietro Bernadone brought Francis before the tribunal of the bishop of Assisi. Asked to return his father's money, Francis stripped off his clothes, threw them at Pietro's feet and cried out: "Listen to me, all of you, and understand! Until now I have called Pietro Bernardone my father. But now I can say: Our Father who is in heaven." Francis broke with his past to begin a new spiritual life. He moved to the oratory of San Damiano where he divided his time between prayer and masonry work. He dressed like a hermit and went from one church to another, with a stick in his hand, to undertake repair work. One day, while attending mass in the *Basilica of Santa Maria degli Angeli* (Saint Mary of the Angels), whose restoration he had just completed, he heard the old priest pronounce these words of Christ: "Go therefore and preach, saying, The kingdom of heaven is at hand. Do not carry in your belongings gold, silver, or coins, nor a bag for the road, nor two tunics, nor sandals, nor a staff." Carried away by these words, Francis threw away his shoes and his staff, keeping only one tunic and decided to adopt the itinerant life of a disciple of Christ. From that day on, he traveled the roads preaching peace and love. Very soon, some rich bourgeois of Assisi joined him. Thus the Franciscan community was born. It will have 5,000 members in 1226. To receive the approval of the Pope, Francis went to Rome with his brothers in 1209, where he obtained an audience with Innocent III. The Pope gave him his oral approval after some hesitation. Recognized as a religious order, the community of penitents in Assisi found new followers, the most famous of whom were Leo, Genevieve, and Masseo. Francis and his brothers claimed a new evangelical way of life, marked by humility, poverty, fraternity, and compassion for all living beings.

> Freed from his disgust and fear to love others as God loved him, Francis proceeded to give away everything he owned and turned his life to the service of the sick and the downcast, for the glory of the Lord. He took it as a matter of courtesy that he should never be in the presence of anyone poorer than himself.[9]

Francis was well aware of all desperations and sufferings in life, but he confronted these burdens with a nonviolent moral courage and a compassionate vision of life. As he treated his fellow human beings so he treated all of his fellow creatures. His great canticle *Laudes Creaturarum* speaks of sun, moon, and water as brothers and sisters. According to his disciple and first biographer Thomas of Celano, "Even towards little worms he glowed with exceeding love," and "used to pick them up in the way and put them in a safe place, that they might not be crushed by the feet of passersby." This was not mere sentimentality but a gratitude grounded in an intimate awareness of the dependency of life. Indeed, on his deathbed he extended his canticle of creation with the words, "Be praised, my Lord, through our Sister Bodily Death, from whose embrace no living person can escape." How, within the creation of an omnipotent and beneficent God, there can be both suffering and love remains a mystery. But clearly for Francis, that creation was simultaneously material and spiritual—sacramental through and through."[10] This compassionate and nonviolent attitude of Saint Francis in relation to all elements of life, including water, wind, and moon, can only be fully appreciated against the backdrop of his famous prayer: "Lord, make me an instrument of your peace. Where there is hatred, let me sow love; where there is injury, pardon; where there is doubt, faith; where there is despair, hope; where there is darkness, light; and where there is sadness, joy."[11] Accordingly, Saint Francis considered love to be the founding principle of spiritual life. This spontaneous and enthusiastic love was accompanied by a humility of spirit and the greatest gentleness towards all living creatures. Thus, to the spirit of poverty was added the cosmic joy. Saint Francis expressed his encounter with nature in hymns of praise for the stars and the flowers. He sang with the birds and showed great love for the

Love and Compassion in Christianity   41

smallest of animals. Thomas of Celano, the first biographer of Saint Francis, evoked this passion in the following words:

> Francis the most blessed servant of God left his companions in the way and ran eagerly toward the birds. When he was come close to them and saw that they were awaiting him, he gave them his accustomed greeting. But, not a little surprised that the birds did not fly away (as they are wont to do) he was filled with exceeding joy and humbly begged them to hear the word of God: and, after saying many things to them he added, "My brother birds, much ought you to praise your Creator, and ever to love Him who has given you feathers for clothing, wings for flight and all that you had need of. God has made you noble among His creatures, for He has given you a habitation in the purity of the air, and, whereas you neither sow nor reap, He himself does still protect and govern you without any care of your own." On this (as he himself and the brethren who had been with him used to say) those little birds, rejoicing in wondrous fashion, after their nature, began to stretch out their necks, to spread their wings, to open their beaks and to gaze on him. And then he went to and fro amidst them, touching their heads and bodies with his tunic. At length he blessed them, and, having. made the sign of the Cross, gave them leave to fly away to another place.[12]

The spiritual message of Saint Francis, then, was more than simple ascetic stripping. It was an experience of Christian nonviolence practiced in the form of communion with the world. In the depth of this communion, Saint Francis opened himself to divine love and to the evangelical joy of salvation, transforming them into a path of praise. To use a formula of Paul Ricoeur, Francis of Assisi was successful to "convert all hostility into fraternal tension, within the unity of creation."[13] For Saint Francis, living and preaching compassion and nonviolence were one. This passion for nonviolence is evident in his *Canticle of the Creatures*, so often quoted, notably by Mother Teresa. As such, Francis of Assisi has entered into legend as the one who came closest to the ideal of compassion of early Christianity and to the teachings of Jesus Christ on nonviolence and love. In his *Testament* Saint Francis reflected on the place of compassion in his life, the legacy that he left behind to all practitioners of principled nonviolence.

The making or showing of compassion was an even more pressing reality in modern times than it was in the early thirteenth century. Actually, two philosophical attitudes in nineteenth century gave shape to the Christian message of Christ on love and compassion. On the one hand, Kierkegaard's existentialist approach to Christian theology had a great impact on writers and thinkers of twentieth century. On the other hand, Tolstoy's mystical Christianity influenced future spiritual leaders of the twentieth century such as Mahatma Gandhi. At the core of Kierkegaard's idea of compassion, we can find the duty to love one's neighbor as oneself. In his seminal religious-philosophical treatise of 1847, entitled *Works of Love*, Kierkegaard distinguishes between neighborly love and preferential love (including romantic love and friendship), and gives priority to the former.

> Kierkegaard draws a clear division here between preferential love and Christian love. The division is defined as follows: erotic love and friendship belong to the category of preferential love, which is characterized by exclusivity ("there is but one and only one beloved") and is based on preference, while the other category— that of Christian love—is characterized by equality ("teaches us to love all people") and is based on self-denial. Christian love is the love expressed in the commandment "You shall love your

neighbour as yourself" (Matthew 22:39), and this "shall," this duty, is "the very mark of Christian love" (Kierkegaard 1995, 24). Christian love is therefore the duty to love the neighbor, any neighbor, as one loves oneself, while preferential love is the love directed at one special neighbor who, by virtue of preference, has a different status than all the other neighbors.[14]

As such, the central point in Kierkegaard's idea of compassionate love was that it is based on self-sacrifice and a willingness to suffer for the Other. *Works of Love* is Kierkegaard's most powerful writing on the concepts of love and compassion. According to Kierkegaard, it is through love and compassionate suffering that singular existences could communicate with each other. Therefore, love of the Other cannot function without trust and belief. Actually, compassion is not giving up hope for the other person. As Kierkegaard asserted:

> Therefore never in unlovingness give up a person or give up hope for him, for it is possible that even the most prodigal son can still be saved, that the most embittered enemy, alas, he who was your friend, it is still possible that he can again become your friend; it is possible that he who was sunk the deepest, alas, because he stood so high, it is still possible that he can be raised up again; it is still possible that the love which has turned cold can burn again—therefore never give up any man, not even at the last moment; do not despair. No, hope all things![15]

In other words, Kierkegaard considered compassionate and responsible love as an existential commitment that denied all reference to a non-humble and self-willful self-love, which was not focused on the otherness of the Other. According to Kierkegaard:

> That love abides is presented, then, as praiseworthy, but as unworthy that it does not abide, that it ceases, that it becomes

altered. Only the first is love; the other by its alteration shows itself not to be love- and consequently that it never was love at all. The case is this, one cannot cease to be loving; if one in truth is loving he continues to be so. If one ceases *to be* loving, then one never *was* loving anyway. Therefore ceasing, in respect to love, has a retroactive power. Yes, I can never become weary of saying and pointing this out: wherever love is, there is something infinitely profound. For example, a man may have had money, and when it is gone, when he no longer has money, it nevertheless remains absolutely true and certain that he *has had* money. But if one ceases to love, he *has never been* loving at all. What is so mild as love and yet so rigorous, so strict with itself, so disciplining as love.[16]

Thus, we can see that for Kierkegaard, not all loving is compassionate love. He considered only neighborly love as the true love. As such, what we can learn from Kierkegaard's Christian existential philosophy is that one cannot cheat oneself out of compassion. Compassion is a form of loving that is not accompanied with self-deception. Therefore, as Kierkegaard argued:

To cheat oneself out of love is the most terrible deception; it is an eternal loss for which there is no reparation, either in time or in eternity. For usually, whatever variations there may be, when there is talk of being deceived in love the one deceived is still related to love, and the deception is simply that it is not present where it was thought to be; but one who is self-deceived has locked himself out and continues to lock himself out from love. There is also talk about being deceived by life or in life; but he who self-deceptively cheated himself out of living—his loss is irredeemable. One who throughout his whole life has been deceived by life—for him the eternal can treasure rich compensation; but the person who has deceived himself has prevented himself from winning the eternal. He who because

Love and Compassion in Christianity 45

of love became sacrifice to human deceit—what has he really lost when in eternity it turns out that love endures; whereas the deception is no more![17]

We quote these passages at length to show Kierkegaard's emphasis on the eternity of love. As a matter of fact, compassion is nothing but the spiritual life of love. That is why compassionate love is a passionate love which is not self-love. For Kierkegaard, the true compassionate love, the neighborly love is the height of understanding the otherness of the Other. As he underlined:

Love of one's neighbour, on the other hand, is self-renouncing love, and self-renunciation casts out all preferential love just as it casts out all self-love-otherwise self-renunciation would also make distinctions and would nourish preference for preference... Christian love also has a one and only object, one's neighbour, but one's neighbour is as far as possible from being only one person, one and only, infinitely removed from this, for one's neighbour is all men.[18]

This exemplifies the development in Kierkegaard's understanding of authentic compassion, while simultaneously interpreting love in self-sacrificial terms. Also, when referring to neighbour, Kierkegaard was actually pointing at all human beings, who are equal before God. Christian compassionate love is directed to all equally. Therefore, according to Kierkegaard:

One's neighbor is one's equal. One's neighbor is not the beloved, for whom you have passionate preference, nor your friend, for whom you have passionate preference. Nor is your neighbor, if you are well educated, the well-educated person with whom you have cultural equality—for with your neighbor you have before God the equality of humanity. Nor is your neighbor one who is of higher social status than you, that is, insofar as he is of higher social status he is not your neighbor, for to love him because he is of higher status than you can very easily be preference and to that extent self-love. Nor is your neighbor one who is inferior to you, that is, insofar as he is inferior he is not your neighbor, for to love one because he is inferior can very easily be partiality's condescension and to that extent self-love. No, to love one's neighbor means equality... [19]

Kierkegaard believed that it is common for all people to exercise preferential love, but that it is uncommon that we exercise equality in loving others. However, we need to remember that by saying this Kierkegaard is basing his views on the teachings of Jesus. Therefore, Christian compassion is the essential love, because for Christianity, love is a matter of conscience. Here, what is important for Kierkegaard is love as the external representation of the inward existence of the individual. He, therefore, argued:

Love is a matter of conscience and thus is not a matter of impulse and inclination or a matter of feeling or a matter of intellectual calculation. According to the secular or purely human point of view many different kinds of live are discernible.... With Christianity the opposite is the case. It recognizes only one kind of love, spiritual love, and does not busy itself very much in elaborating on the different ways in which this essentially common love can reveal itself. All distinctions between the many different kinds of love are essentially abolished by Christianity.[20]

In all and for all in Kierkegaard's philosophy, compassionate love was neither erotic, nor friendly love. From his point of view, compassion was a matter of conscience and indebtedness to the Other. Here, we find a concept unfolded by Kierkegaard, which will also be used by Martin Luther King, Jr. in his philosophy

Love and Compassion in Christianity 47

of nonviolence. According to Kierkegaard, the true lover is in "infinite debt" to the neighbor.

> And what must be done in order to be in the debt of love to each other? When a fisherman has caught a fish in his net and wishes to keep it alive, what must he do? He must immediately put it in water; otherwise it becomes exhausted and dies after a time. And why must he put it in water? Because water is the fish's element, and *everything which shall be kept alive must be kept in its element.* But love's element is infinitude, inexhaustibility, immeasurability. If you will keep your love, then, by the help of debt's infinitude, imprisoned in freedom and life, you must take care that it continually remains in its element... .But what can take love out of its element? *As soon as love concentrates upon itself it is out of its element.* What does that mean, to concentrate upon itself? It means to become an object for itself. But an *object* is like a finite fixed point, a boundary, a stopping-place, a dangerous thing for infinitude. Love can never *infinitely* become its own object; nor is their danger in that. For *infinitely* to be an object for itself is to remain in infinitude and thus, simply by existing or continuing to exist (since love is a reduplication in itself) is as different from the particularity of natural life as is the reduplication of the spirit. Consequently, if love *concentrates* upon itself, it must become an object for itself in its individual expression, or another and separate love becomes its object, love in this person and love in that person. When the object is thus finite, love concentrates on itself, for *infinitely* to concentrate on itself means precisely a becoming. But when love finitely concentrates on itself, everything is lost....[Love] becomes for itself an object, which, more accurately defined, is *comparison.* Love cannot *infinitely* compare itself with itself, for infinite self-comparison would only be a way of saying that it is itself; in such an infinite comparison there is no third factor; love is a reduplication and therefore there is no comparison. All comparison requires a third factor together

with similarity and dissimilarity.... But what can comparison's third factor be? A person can compare his love with the love of another.... The moment of comparison is a selfish moment, a moment which wants to be *for* itself....[This sort of] love expects *by way of comparison* to get status in relationship to others' love or in relationship to its own achievements.... To love *by way of comparison* more than all other men, even if this were the case, is: not to love. To love is to remain in infinite debt; the infinitude of the debt is the bond of perfection.[21]

Finally, it should be added that Kierkegaard's position on the concept of Christian love reveals his deep commitment to interconnect existential ontology and an interpretation of compassion. By doing this, he remained a Christian philosopher, rather than being tempted to walk in the world of Christian mysticism like Leo Tolstoy.

Tolstoy's career as a Christian thinker and a social reformer was exemplified by his devotion to Jesus's doctrine of love and nonviolence in the last thirty years of his life. In many respects, Tolstoy should be considered as the great apostle of nonviolence in the nineteenth century. However, many did not consider him as a serious thinker even if they admired him for his talent as a great writer. Bertrand Russell, for example, in a 1904 letter to Lowes Dickinson, expressed admiration for Tolstoy's ethical positions, but concluded: "It is the greatest misfortune to the human race that he [Tolstoy] has so little power of reasoning."[22] As for Isaiah Berlin, he echoed the opinion of a nineteenth-century Russian critic, Mikhailovsky, and wrote: "Two things are always said about Count Tolstoy, that he is an outstandingly good writer of fiction and a bad thinker."[23] More than 112 years after the death of the Russian writer, critics and historians of ideas are still divided on

Love and Compassion in Christianity   49

his true genius as a Christian thinker of nonviolence. Perhaps we should see here the mark of a complex personality. On the one hand, Tolstoy the writer, who was curious about everything and taking pleasure in painting the Russian society of his time. On the other hand, Tolstoy the Christian mystic and moralist who was against the Russian Tsarist state and the Russian Orthodox Church. "Moreover, Tolstoy recognized that simple people had certain qualities that the more educated and spoiled classes lacked, and vice versa (...) Tolstoy immersed himself in the study of philosophy and theology, which eventually resulted in his conversion, an event that William James famously described as an attempt at self-cure on the part of a 'sick' and divided soul."[24] Tolstoy adhered to Pascal's religious thought and the true essence of Christian thought. He discovered in Pascal, a new definition of knowledge by faith inscribed in the heart of man, which is opposed and differentiated from knowledge by reason. This philosophical interrogation followed by his reflections on the nature of power, that he undertook while writing his famous novels, *War and Peace* and *Anna Karenina*, provided the theoretical basis for Tolstoy's principle of Christian nonviolence. Following the teachings of Jesus and the evangelical postulate, Tolstoy believed that the essence of human life is love and he considered ecclesiastical Christianity and the rule of the Church as the direct distortion of the teachings of Christ. "What Tolstoy considered the beacons on a Christian's spiritual way [were] the commandments given by Christ in the *Sermon on the Mount* among which the most important, from his viewpoint, was the commandment 'do not resist evil' which Tolstoy and his followers interpreted as the inadmissibility of resisting evil by violence."[25] Evil, in Tolstoy's mind, stemmed only from the function of modern religious and political institutions.

50 *Comparative Approaches to Compassion*

Through the life of the characters in his novels, Tolstoy showed clearly that institutions like the Church and the State did not follow the lessons of love and compassion of Jesus Christ. Therefore, in reaction to the spirit of his time, Tolstoy defined his new moral mission as service to God and to the teachings of Jesus Christ.

The old Tolstoy came to the conclusion that in order to serve God, one must serve one's fellow human beings, for God demands only love and compassion from us. Tolstoy constantly advocated the doctrine of worship by deeds that he had discovered in the Gospels. The teaching of Christ appeared to him as the cornerstone of all moral and political actions and the only weapon that allowed human beings to overcome the absurd obstacle of death and to fight against the lies and hypocrisy of political power. Therefore, far from propagating a new theological dogma, Tolstoy undertook a new social critique based on faith. In obedience to the truth of Christ, he preached the disaffection of power, sending back to back political power and authority of the Church that he accused both of corrupting the people. He urged people around the world to understand that they belonged to God before belonging to a state. Therefore:

> The love of neighbor, which the Church propagated as an essential value of Christianity, was not difficult when it had to be applied to a friend or a person who did not endanger either one's own life or one's own interests. But [for Tolstoy] it was in the love of one's enemy that it really showed its full extent and was put to the test. Thus, love of neighbor was crystallized for Tolstoy in the Christian commandment of non-resistance against evil, which the Russian writer translated into the idea of nonviolence.[26]

As such, Tolstoy tried to strengthen the Christian faith by the way of love and nonviolence. But he also believed that only the ethic of love, as described by Jesus and the Apostles, was capable of grounding an ideal nonviolent community.

In his commitment to a mystic quest for Christian love and compassion, and his passion for nonviolent transformation of the world, Thomas Merton's life and thought reveal remarkable similarities to Tolstoy's. Merton was converted to Roman Catholicism, few years after entering a monastic order of his church, and finally became an ordained priest. However, the Tolstoy–Merton connection is less a matter of direct influence of the former on the latter, than that of an intellectual affinity that both men had with Mohandas Karamchand Gandhi. Tolstoy and Merton never met Gandhi, but they both respected the man and his ideas. Gandhi was particularly influenced by Tolstoy's book *The Kingdom of God Is Within You* and corresponded with him in 1909, while he was writing his seminal book *Hind Swaraj* and having success with his *Satyagraha* movement in South Africa. As for Merton, while it would be simplistic to consider him as a follower of Gandhian nonviolence, clearly there are enough points to talk about Gandhi's inspiring role in the making of Merton's social philosophy. As a Christian pacifist and an admirer of Martin Luther King, Jr. and the civil rights movement in America, Merton was well aware of the iconic figure of Gandhi as a prophet of nonviolence. "In looking to Gandhi as the preeminent modern teacher and practitioner of nonviolent resistance to social injustice and war"[27] he also recognized the role played by Tolstoy and Thoreau in the development of Gandhi's philosophy of nonviolence.

In the introduction to his book of selections from Gandhi, Merton wrote, "It was through his acquaintance with writers like Tolstoy and Thoreau, and then his reading of the New Testament, that Gandhi rediscovered his own tradition.... One

52   *Comparative Approaches to Compassion*

of the great lessons of Gandhi's life remains this: through the spiritual traditions of the West he, an Indian, discovered his Indian heritage and with it his own 'right mind.'"[28]

The central dynamic of Merton's contemplative life as a monk belonging to the Order of Cistercians of the Strict Observance (*Trappists*) was his love of God and neighbor. For Merton, authentic love required solitude. In this regard, he argued:

> Who knows anything at all about solitude if he has not been in love, and in love in his solitude. Love and solitude must trust each other in the man who means to live alone: they must become one and the same thing in him, or he will only be half a person. Unless I have you with me always, in some very quiet and perfect way, I will never be able to live fruitfully alone.[29]

As in the case of Saint Francis, for Thomas Merton love and compassion was not limited to human beings, but it concerned all of God's creatures. He considered loving living beings as feeling the very presence of God in nature. "For Merton, Gospel spirituality was, again, an incarnational spirituality. It was, therefore, rooted in Christ and focused on the liberation of every human being from every denigration and degradation."[30] As such, Merton emphasized on love, compassion and friendship as necessary paths to attain spiritual development and cultivate an inter-cultural and environmental understanding. "Thus, for Merton, to be part of society inevitably meant not only being part of a particular political and social system, but also....[looking] toward a society dominated by the personality of Christ."[31] Merton's contemplation of Jesus as a compassionate prophet and his search for God through all living things was an effort to balance philosophy of nonviolence and struggle for social justice. As he wrote in his book *Seeds of Destruction* (1964), "The contemplative life is not, and cannot be, a mere withdrawal, a pure negation, a turning of one's back on the world with its sufferings, its crises, its confusions and its errors."[32] It would be interesting to point out that Thomas Merton was fully conscious about the fact that Gandhi venerated the figure of Christ. Moreover, Merton was persuaded (and he was correct) that the Christian model of nonviolent struggle appealed to Gandhi as a mode of thought that resolved the tension between contemplation and action. Let us not forget that there was more than a simple reminder of Gandhian philosophy in Merton's Christian nonviolence. "Said Merton once, praising Gandhi's ethics: 'To conform is not to act well, but only to "look good" — highlighting the difference between insincere pious behavior and "genuinely ethical conduct.""[33]

Thomas Merton tried to come to grips with the conflict between his vocation as a Trappist contemplative monk and his search for love and contemplation in other forms of spirituality, notably those of the East.

> God, a God who is the epitome of creativity and freedom— an existentialist God. For Merton the divine existentialism had been illuminated by Christ, who manifested the kind of existence God has a sacrificial, generous, and loving sharing of being that contrasts with the bleak existentialism set forth by Sartre. In the case of those religious contemplatives who approached being with other than Christian eyes, Merton saw a similar divine compassion radiating from the center of existence—as in his startling view in 1968 of the great stone Buddhas in Polonnaruwa, Sri Lanka, whose expression, he wrote, conveyed an inexhaustible "emptiness" and "compass."[34]

54   *Comparative Approaches to Compassion*

All of this was also consistent with Merton's interest in the reality of the spiritual as the presence and vibrancy of love. As a matter of fact, Merton's advocacy of Christian love and compassion provided him with a starting point for understanding the essence of contemplative life as a way of loving. He wrote:

> Contemplation is the work of love, and the contemplative proves his love by leaving all things, even the most spiritual things, for God in nothingness, detachment, and "night." But the deciding factor in contemplation is the free and unpredictable action of God. He alone can grant the gift of mystical grace and make Him self known by the secret, ineffable contact that reveals His presence in the depths of the soul. What counts is not the soul's love for God, but God's love for the soul.[35]

What Merton's life as a whole demonstrated was that Christian attitude toward compassion and love is an effort to integrate human life into a single moral whole. And that is a fundamental point that we can find in Gandhi's approach to love, compassion, and nonviolence in both explicit and implicit ways.

3

Mahatma Gandhi: Compassionate Citizenship and Feminization of Politics

No Christian thinker other than Tolstoy had a deep moral and political influence in early twentieth century. Yet today, many around the world are interested in Tolstoy's message of love and resistance against evil, because of its impact on the young Mohandas Karamchand Gandhi, a Hindu with a Christian heart. Mahatma Gandhi was neither a saint nor a preacher. More than anything else, he was a spiritual dissenter in search of justice and in quest of Truth. Till the end of his life, Gandhi considered himself a follower of Tolstoy and he recommended to his fellow Indians to read the books of the Russian sage. Actually, one can say that Tolstoy was the only Christian thinker who impressed Gandhi and introduced him correctly to the teachings of Jesus on love and compassion. Gandhi wrote: "Tolstoy's *The Kingdom of God Is Within You* overwhelmed me. It left an abiding impression on me. Before the independent thinking, profound morality, and the truthfulness of this book, all the books given me by Mr. Coates seemed to pale into insignificance."[1] What attracted Gandhi in the Christian message of Tolstoy was the simple and compassionate character of Jesus himself. However, Gandhi was far from being interested in the Christian theological debates and despite the efforts of his Christian friends, he refused to be converted into Christianity. As he affirmed in his *Autobiography*:

56 Comparative Approaches to Compassion

I saw no reason for changing my belief -my religion. It was impossible for me to believe that I could go to heaven or attain salvation only by becoming a Christian. When I frankly said so to some of the good Christian friends, they were shocked. But there was no help for it. My difficulties lay deeper. It was more than I could believe that Jesus was the only incarnate son of God, and that only he who believed in him would have everlasting life. If God could have sons, all of us were His sons. If Jesus was like God, or God Himself, then all men were like God and could be God Himself. My reason was not ready to believe literally that Jesus by his death and by his blood redeemed the sins of the world. Metaphorically there might be some truth in it. Again, according to Christianity only human beings had souls, and not other living beings, for whom death meant complete extinction; while I held a contrary belief. I could accept Jesus as a martyr, an embodiment of sacrifice, and a divine teacher, but not as the most perfect man ever born. His death on the Cross was a great example to the world, but that there was anything like a mysterious or miraculous virtue in it my heart could not accept. The pious lives of Christians did not give me anything that the lives of men of other faiths had failed to give. I had seen in other lives just the same reformation that I had heard of among Christian principles. From the point of view of sacrifice, it seemed to me that the Hindus greatly surpassed the Christians. It was impossible for me to regard Christianity as a perfect religion or the greatest of all religions.[2]

Consequently, in Gandhi's view, Jesus was a *satyagrahi*, in the same way as Socrates, who became a martyr in his quest for Truth and justice. Looking at Jesus as a teacher of love, compassion, and *ahimsa* was also for Gandhi a way to emphasize on the idea of "sacrifice" (*yajna*) which was a point of rapprochement between the *Bhagavad Gita* and the *New Testament*. According to Gandhi,

Mahatma Gandhi 57

"Jesus put on a crown of thorns to win salvation for his people, allowed his hands and feet to be nailed and suffered agonies before he gave up the ghost. This has been the law of yajna from immemorial times, without yajna the earth cannot exist even for a moment."[3] It goes without saying that the notion of "sacrifice" is one of the basic principles behind Gandhian philosophy of *Satyagraha* and his life-sustaining ideal of *Sarvodaya*. Accordingly, Gandhi saw a relation between the two principles of compassion and self-sacrifice. He considered Jesus Christ, in the same way as the Buddha, as epitomes of gentleness and love. For Gandhi,

> even as the Buddha and Christ chastised they showed unmistakable gentleness and love behind every act of theirs. They would not raise a finger against their enemies, but would gladly surrender themselves rather than the truth for which they lived. The Buddha would have died resisting the priesthood, if the majesty of his love had not proved to be equal to the task of bending the priesthood. Christ died on the cross with a crown of thorns on his head, defying the might of a whole empire. And if I raise resistances of a nonviolent character, I simply and humbly follow in the footsteps of the great teachers... [4]

What emerged from Gandhi's comparison between the Buddha and Jesus Christ was twofold: on the one hand, Gandhi made the point clear that self-sacrifice (*tapasya*) is *conditio sine qua non* of nonviolent action. On the other hand, he insisted on the fact that one could not live a truly spiritual life of compassion and love without taking part in civic and political actions which served the needs of humanity. Far from having an eschatological approach to the question of love and compassion, Gandhi looked at nonviolence as an unfailing mode of struggle to change the world *hic et nunc* (here and now).

58   *Comparative Approaches to Compassion*

Mahatma Gandhi was well aware that in the process of listening to and learning from other religions he could become more committed to his own Hinduism, while distancing himself from its weaknesses. Of course, this kind of learning required seeing life and love from the perspective of other traditions. As a pilgrim of compassion and love, Gandhi drank deeply from different spiritual wells (either Islam, Buddhism, or Christianity), in order to give a meaning and purpose to his nonviolent vision of the world. Gandhi always described religion as a tree with many branches. He, therefore, did not narrow down his quest of Truth and his search for love and compassion to only one religion. For him living with the otherness of Others was not only a question of harmony and compromise, but also comprehending the suffering of the Other. As such, Gandhi did not envision nonviolence as a political instrument, but as a compassionate state of mind marked by relating to others in their suffering and promoting the moral courage to replace hatred and revenge by kindness and hope. Ultimately, from Gandhi's point of view, nonviolence could not function as a strategy of change without being at the same time an empathetic and compassionate understanding of the Other, motivated by a spirit of dialogue and cooperation. Gandhi claimed to have practiced this compassionate understanding throughout most of his life and to have applied it in all difficult moments of crisis. "My life is made up of compromises," he said, "but they have been compromises that have brought me nearer the goal."[5] As Truth and nonviolence were closely intertwined, in the eyes of Gandhi, like two sides of a coin, so were compassion and inter-faith dialogue. As Gandhi affirmed:

It is a tragedy that religion for us means today nothing more than restrictions on food and drink, nothing more than adherence to a sense of superiority and inferiority. Let me tell you that there cannot be any grosser ignorance than this. Birth and observance of forms cannot determine one's superiority and inferiority. Character is the only determining factor. God did not create men with the badge of superiority or inferiority; no scripture which labels a human being as inferior or untouchable because of his or her birth can command our allegiance, it is a denial of God and Truth which is God.[6]

Gandhi's openness to the plurality of religions was essentially based on the fact that he worshiped God as Truth, and Truth was an unattainable horizon. As Gandhi maintained:

If we had attained the full vision of Truth, we would no longer be mere seekers, but have become one with God, for Truth is God. But being only seekers, we prosecute our quest, and are conscious of our imperfection. And if we are imperfect ourselves, religion as conceived by us must also be imperfect. We have not realized religion in its perfection, even as we have not realized God. Religion of our conception, being thus imperfect, is always subject to a process of evolution. And if all faiths outlined by men are imperfect, the question of comparative merit does not arise. All faiths constitute a revelation of Truth, but all are imperfect, and liable to error. Reverence for other faiths need not blind us to their faults. We must be keenly alive to the defects of our own faith also, yet not leave it on that account, but try to overcome those defects. Looking at all religions with an equal eye, we would not only not hesitate, but would think it our duty, to blend into our faith every acceptable feature of other faiths.[7]

As a man of nonviolence, Gandhi was also a supporter of harmonious exchange among different traditions of thought and a keeper of the flame of empathetic pluralism. Gandhi's conception of empathetic pluralism took on the task of fostering a compassionate understanding of the otherness of the Other, but also bringing

60   *Comparative Approaches to Compassion*

about togetherness and solidarity among individuals and nations. Therefore, as in the case of truth and nonviolence, compassion and communal unity were, for Gandhi, interchangeable entities beyond cultural borders and mental ghettos. Gandhi's faith in the eternal essence of Indian civilization was based on the optimistic vision (though not an unrealistic one), that Hindus and Muslims could construct together a nonviolent social order in India. As he explained:

> The British have made themselves believe that they are ruling because of our quarrels, and that they will gladly retire when we have ceased to quarrel. The British rule must be permanent if the adjustment of the communal quarrel is a condition precedent to India becoming independent. It is a purely domestic problem which we are bound to solve if we are to live at peace with one another. May I remind the critic and those who argue like him that only a short while ago it was said that if the British withdrew, Hindus would be left to the mercy of the virile races from the north, that not a virgin would be safe or a monied man retain his wealth? Now Princes and Muslims, who are able enough to protect themselves against unarmed millions whom the Congress claims specially to represent, are sought to be protected by the British bayonet against the latter! Be that as it may, the congress must pursue its even course. It must work for communal unity in spite of odds against it. It is a plank in its programme. It is part of the nonviolent technique.[8]

As evident, what is special and original in Gandhian thought is the ethics of love and a spirit of genuine reciprocity and mutuality. The heart of Gandhi's ethics of interconnectedness was to look within oneself, while looking at the Other. "Gandhi, as a true karma yogin would insist that detached, selfless action, which derives from a true knowledge of the Self, is action in the service of humanity, and also to seek the welfare of all men both springs from, and leads to, the realization of one's identity with all that lives and to the realization of Truth or God."[9] At a more philosophical level, in Gandhi's view, every person could and should learn from others. As a result, for Gandhi, non-violent organization of society is a matter of belief in the essential unity of all citizens. In other words, the empathetic unity and interconnectedness of human lives is such that the selfless role of compassionate individuals has an enduring impact on the destiny of the whole community and on that of the world. As Gandhi famously said:

> I do not believe that an individual may gain spiritually and those that surround him suffer. I believe in *advaita*. I believe in the essential unity of man and for that matter of all that lives. Therefore, I believe that if one man gains spiritually, the whole world gains with him and, if one man falls, the whole world falls to that extent.[10]

Gandhi, in the manner of the Buddha and Jesus, believed that nonviolence is the external worldly manifestation of love and compassion as eternal spiritual principles. He sought, therefore, to project the ethic of compassion to the center of social and political life. Given his insistence on the interconnectedness of all departments of life, Mahatma Gandhi was absolutely convinced that the human world was a vast mosaic of suffering souls which needed moral transformation and social change in order to survive. But Gandhi also knew that this social change would require a revaluation of values and priorities. Therefore, far from turning to the human capacity to pity, Gandhi searched for the ultimate measure of human dignity and its more noble life in the concept of compassion. Like Jesus Christ and the Buddha, his altruism was extravagant and dangerous, but it was a magnificent expression of moral resistance and political dissent. As such, Gandhi's spiritual and moral belief in the compassionate interdependence of all human beings led him to see women as the pillars of the human family and the vanguards of social change in the world. Therefore, apart from being a social reformer to the core, Gandhi rose to eminence for his views on justice and equality for women and the feminine nature of politics.

Gandhi challenged much of the traditional values and orthodox teachings of the Indian society concerning women. As a result, not only he encouraged the Indian women to have a significant role in the nonviolent struggle for independence against the British Raj, but he also took the first steps to rethink the notion of politics away from its traditional masculine and paternalistic nature. After his return to India in 1915, Gandhi challenged many of the customs and institutions in India which targeted women and violated their individual rights, such as child marriage, veil (purdah), burning of widows (sati), temple prostitution (devadasi), and illiteracy. But he was also very concerned by the political role of Indian women and their moral asset in the *Satyagraha* movement.

> Women like Sarladevi Chaudhrani, Oliver Schriner, Millie Graham Polock, Sucheta Kripalani, Anasuyaben Sarabahi, Aruna Asaf Ali, Durgabai Deshmukh, Begum Hasrat Mohani, Avantikabai Gokhale and the Faizi sisters, to name some, were pioneering new avenues for women—in education, women's participation in politics and widow remarriage. They were quick to organise meetings for Gandhi as he travelled the length and breadth of India to understand the most prevalent issues of the day.[11]

In support of the cause of women, Gandhi went so far as to praise women's capacity for nonviolence. He argued: "If non-violence is the law of our being, the future is with woman."[12] What is indicated here by Gandhi's insistence on the future of humanity being in the hands of women is simply what can be called the process of feminization of modern politics. The core of Gandhi's theory of politics is to show that the compassionate and empathetic citizen is the true political subject and not the violent state. As such, the political subject's decision on sovereignty becomes, for Gandhi, the true subject of political sovereignty. As a result, the Gandhian moment of politics is an effort to de-masculinize the concept of modern politics as presented by the omnipotent sovereign of Thomas Hobbes and the Hegelian state. From the Gandhian point of view, the opposition here is not only between violence and nonviolence, but also between moral power and political power. Accordingly, in the eyes of Gandhi women represent the moral power and the virtue of compassion against the patriarchal state. As he underlined:

Passive resistance is regarded as the weapon of the weak, but the resistance for which I had to coin a new name altogether is the weapon of the strongest. I had to coin a new word to signify what I meant. But its matchless beauty lies in the fact that, though it is the weapon of the strongest, it can be wielded by the weak in body, by the aged, and even by the children if they have stout hearts. And since resistance in *Satyagraha* is offered through self-suffering, it is a weapon pre-eminently open to women. We found last year that women in India, in many instances, surpassed their brothers in sufferings and the two played a noble part in the campaign. For the ideal of self-suffering became contagious and they embarked upon amazing acts of self-denial. Supposing that the women and the children of Europe became fired with the love of humanity, they would take the men by storm and reduce militarism to nothingness in an incredibly short time. The underlying idea is that women, children and others have the same soul, the same potentiality. The question is one of drawing out the limitless power of truth.[13]

It is interesting how Gandhi constructs a moral connection between the act of self-sacrifice and womanhood. One should keep in mind that for Gandhi self-sacrifice is the prerogative of the *satyagrahi* who practices love and compassionate understanding. Gandhi, in underlining the ethical demands of nonviolence recognized the universal capability of the feminine to tenderness and love. As such, Gandhi reflected on the moral duty of the Indian citizen's struggle under the light of the feminine essence of nonviolence. Consequently, he projected a future for the Indian society in which "all disabilities attaching to women, in regard to public employment, office of power or honor, etc."[14] were abolished. As such, there was no sexual segregation in the Gandhian approach to politics and "gender boundaries crumbled as men were nudged towards work that women were meant to do. [For example], the spinning wheel was compulsory for both, as was a reorientation of domestic consumption. Both were trained to face aggression without retaliation, which was the way 'virtuous' women traditionally behaved in the face of domestic tyranny."[15]

Because Gandhi conceived of India's identity as nonviolent and compassionate, he made women an integral part of the process of ethicalization of politics.

> *Satyagraha* linked the national movement to every home in India. Women could connect and become an integral part of the movement. Gandhi wanted to awaken, in as many minds of as many women as possible, a consciousness of their present condition, as well as stir them to patriotism and encourage them

Mahatma Gandhi

to fight "shoulder to shoulder" with the men against the Raj, and to join the Indian National Congress.23 Having pulled women out of passivity to active participation, he was at first reluctant to completely challenge certain traditional gender stereotypes. For example, he submerged many women's issues like family planning by promoting abstinence instead. But the women, who had by now begun to enjoy their new-found freedoms, realised that they did not have to accept the norms of male-dominated politics. They evolved their own perspectives and formulated their own methods.[16]

That is to say, the Gandhian feminization of Indian politics led at the same time to the entry of women in the Indian public sphere and to undifferentiated regime of self-governance. Yet, one should be careful not to turn Gandhi into a god-like leader who solved all the gender problems in India. It is true that Gandhi, in the manner of Tolstoy, was so preoccupied by his own spiritual quest and his personal conception of the *brahmacharya* that he denied the sexual needs of his wife, Kasturba, but as Sujata Patel points out correctly, Gandhi took an

enormous leap by giving a significant role to women in contemporary Indian society... [He] also made women into a subject, making her realise that she had freedom, qualities and attributes which are crucial to contemporary society. In a radical re-construction, he gave her confidence in herself and in her essence. He made woman realise that she has a significant and a dominant role to play in the family, that both she and her husband are equal and that within the family they both have similar rights. In a path breaking intervention, he made possible not only the involvement of women in politics, but made her realise that the national movement could not succeed without her involvement in the struggle. Gandhi ultimately empowered woman in the family and in marriage.[17]

However, what still remains today as Gandhi's response to the lack of compassion and kindness in our everyday politics around the world was his effort to reinvigorate Indian public life and beyond by thinking and living politics from the "feminine" perspective of nonviolence. Gandhi was first and foremost a "feminine" social reformer and politician who understood politics in terms of radical compassion in freedom and radical freedom in compassion. To put it differently, we can say that for Gandhi, thinking politics in its feminine nature was an unconditional act of love and compassion. As a moral leader and a political sage, Gandhi ensured women's fair access to the political sphere as self-governing citizens, making gender equality measures central to public policymaking in India. Surely, by his nonviolent strategy and his belief in the feminization process of the public sphere, Gandhi turned Indian women into agents of nationalism. He also identified himself with women and defined *Swaraj* in terms of their chores in everyday life, like spinning, weaving, and cleaning. For Gandhi, caring for the situation of women in India seemed to be a moral prelude to political equality and civic friendship between men and women. Therefore, Gandhi considered nonviolence as the public exercise of the ethic of empathy and an urgent response to male superiority in the Hindu tradition. As a matter of fact, Gandhi's strategy was to maintain the unity of the Indian society, while undermining and subverting gender inequality present in Hindu society. Gandhi dared to criticize and disobey traditional restrictions of Indian women, as part of his larger struggle to feminize the political grammar of Indians. He knew well that the key to the upliftment and empowerment of women in India would be their proper education. He wrote:

> I believe in the proper education of women. But I do believe that woman will not make her contribution to the world by mimicking

or running a race with men. She can run the race, but she will not rise to the great heights she is capable of by mimicking man.... Woman is the companion of man gifted with equal mental capacities. She has the right to participate in the minutest detail of the activities of man, and she has the same right of freedom and liberty as he. She is entitled to a supreme place in her own sphere of activity as man is in his. This ought to be the natural condition of things, and not a result only of learning to read and write. By sheer force of a vicious custom, even the most ignorant and wordless men have been enjoying a superiority over women which they do not deserve and ought not to have.[18]

It must be noted that Gandhi's feminization of politics in India was much more than just a straightforward strategy to win the national struggle for independence. If that was the case, he would have never been assassinated by Nathuram Godse. According to Godse, one of the reasons for assassinating Gandhi was: "The way he brought the masses, along with the purdah-clad, homebound women of the country, into the folds of freedom struggle."[19] It is interesting that Godse wanted Hinduism to be masculine and powerful, in order to be able to retaliate to its enemies. Godse considered Gandhi as

the effeminate Father of the Nation who was unable to protect Mother India... Gandhi represented the affirmation of the feminine self, long enshrined in the Hindu ideal of the *ardhnarishwar* (a composite, androgynous divine form, half-male, half-female). This reflected in the deeper divide. Like Savarkar, Godse looked up to the European ideal of centralised, uniform nation-state. Gandhi wanted decentered power and accommodation of differences, even beyond the boundaries of the recently constituted Indian nation. Brahmanic Hinduism was Godse's ideal.[20]

Godse was right. Once Gandhi was eliminated, power politics could take over. India has been independent for seventy-five years based on electoral liberalism in the name of Gandhi. But for more than seventy-five years, Indian political parties have distanced themselves from Gandhi's legacy. Considering the profound spiritual nature of Gandhi's personality and his deep ethical view of politics, we could say that if he was among us today, he would have been troubled by the uncompassionate and un-empathetic essence of politics in today's world. Assuredly, it is important to grasp Gandhi's character above all as a man who, in the manner of Buddha, Jesus, and Mahavira remained all through his life as a person truthful to the ethic of love and compassion, but also to its practice in the domain of politics. In a sense, then, Gandhi's feminine view of nonviolent organization of the society started where the male chauvinistic and macho affirmation of power, greed, and violence ended. Undoubtedly, Gandhi's nonviolence was deeply rooted in the lesson of love and compassion that he had learned from the spiritual leaders of human history. As a result, he knew well that "those who seek to destroy men rather than manners, adopt the latter and become worse than those whom they destroy under the mistaken belief that the manners will die with the men."[21] Those, like Martin Luther King, Jr., and Khan Abdul Ghaffar Khan, who followed the Gandhian message of nonviolence, understood that "Along the way of life, someone must have sense enough and morality enough to cut off the chain of hate. This can only be done by projecting the ethic of love to the center of our lives."[22]

4

The Twin Heritage of Gandhian Nonviolence: Martin Luther King, Jr. and Khan Abdul Ghaffar Khan

Mahatma Gandhi viewed the world as a diverse and pluralist mosaic of interconnected beliefs and actions that demanded compassion, love, duty, and solidarity in order to survive. Gandhi's support of the poor, oppressed, and the pariahs worldwide was noticeable long before his return to India in 1915 and his full engagement as the "Mahatma" (the great soul) in the Indian independence movement. What Gandhi had learned from his intellectual and existential encounters with Jainism, Buddhism, Hinduism, the Gospels, and through his readings of Leo Tolstoy, Henry David Thoreau, John Ruskin, and many others, shaped his mode of thinking and produced his philosophy of nonviolence. Thus, Gandhi's life and message went beyond merely making India free and independent. Significantly, after his assassination, Gandhi was considered as the modern prophet of nonviolence, who had no other ambitions in life but to bring ethics into everyday politics around the world, and to establish effectively the ideals of freedom, equality, and justice. An important part of Gandhi's epoch-making impact on contemporary social and political movements can be studied and analyzed through lives and struggles of men and women who followed his nonviolent path. Admittedly, the spiritual legacy of Gandhi can be found in many great figures of the twentieth century, such as Nelson Mandela, His Holiness the

Dalai Lama, Archbishop Desmond Tutu, and Vaclav Havel, but undoubtedly the two spiritual heirs of Mahatma Gandhi were Reverend Martin Luther King, Jr. and Khan Abdul Ghaffar Khan. The name of Dr. King and his famous speech, "I Have a Dream," is well known to many around the globe, but very few people have heard the name of Khan Abdul Ghaffar Khan, and do know him as a Muslim proponent of nonviolence, who stressed the compatibility of Islam and *Satyagraha*. "Although Ghaffar Khan's independent spirit and aversion to violence pre-dated contact with Mohandas Gandhi, Ghaffar Khan's belief in nonviolence and commitment to social reform were strongly buttressed and further inspired by Gandhi. Ghaffar Khan's rejection of violence was at least as deeply rooted in his Muslim religious faith as was Gandhi's in his Hindu tradition."[1] Inspired by Mahatma Gandhi, Abdul Ghaffar Khan was an unheralded Muslim activist whose work for Indian independence answers those today who doubt the viability of nonviolent Islamic protest.

Khan Abdul Ghaffar Khan was a Pashtun political and spiritual leader who opposed British rule in India. Khan had personally witnessed the maltreatment of a British Raj officer toward a native and having observed numerous failed attempts to oust the British Raj, he decided to organize people into a social activist group called the *Khudai Khidmatgar* (Servants of God) whose goals were initially focused on education and the elimination of blood feuds, but then changed in focus on one specific political goal: the removal of the British Raj. The British Army performed a number of violent and gruesome tactics to destroy the *Khudai Khidmatgar* including throwing people into ponds in the winter time, shaving people's beards, blocking roads, incarcerating protestors, divide-and-rule tactics, poisoning food supplies, and bombing villages.[2]

The Twin Heritage of Gandhian Nonviolence

In response to the violence of the British army, Abdul Ghaffar Khan argued:

There is an answer to violence, which is more violence. But nothing can conquer nonviolence. You cannot kill it. It keeps standing up. The British sent their horses and cars to run over us, but I took my shawl in my mouth to keep from screaming. We were human beings, but we should not cry or express in any way that we were injured or weak.[3]

A compassionate Muslim and a skillful nonviolent strategist, Ghaffar Khan improved his tactics of civil disobedience by involving women in his anti-colonial movement. This greatly demoralized the British Army and reduced their ability to violently attack the Pashtuns. As a matter of fact, members of the *Garwhal Rifles* (light infantry of the Indian Army) refused to fire on nonviolent *Khudai Khidmatgar* protestors in the Peshawar struggle in 1930 and by doing so, sent a clear message to London that the Indian army could not be relied upon to execute orders coming from the British officers. In 1931, the *Khudai Khidmatgar* partnered with the Indian National Congress which forced the British Army to ease their attacks and after a long struggle, in 1937 the *Khudai Khidmatgar* finally attained political power and introduced a number of reforms including land reforms, the teaching of the Pashto language in schools, and the release of political prisoners. "The *Khudai Khidmatgar* movement was not just a political movement. It was also a spiritual movement. It taught the Pathans love and brotherhood that inspired them with a sense of unity, patriotism and the desire to service."[4]

Many historians of modern India have ignored the fact that Khan Abdul Ghaffar Khan was among the few Muslim collaborators of Gandhi who introduced him to a tolerant and nonviolent interpretation of this religion. Gandhi had a very high esteem for Islam and regarded it as a religion of peace, love, and kindness, in the same sense as Christianity, Buddhism and Hinduism. As for Abdul Ghaffar Khan, nonviolence and compassion were key components of his tolerant Islam. Like Gandhi, Ghaffar Khan believed in nonviolence as an article of faith. Nonviolence for him was a moral imperative, not an expedient principle. His compassionate view of religion and politics already predisposed him for being the leader of a nonviolent movement. Yet, it was Gandhi who gave Ghaffar Khan the idea that his compassionate Islam could become a weapon of nonviolence against the British domination. Ghaffar Khan declared:

> Surely there is nothing surprising in a Muslim or a Pathan like me subscribing to this creed. It is not a new creed. It was followed fourteen hundred years ago by the Prophet, all the time he was in Mecca. And it has since been followed by all those who wanted to throw off the oppressor's yoke. But we had so far forgotten it that when Mahatma Gandhi placed it before us, we thought that he was sponsoring a new creed or a novel weapon.[5]

It is worth noting that Ghaffar Khan was different from most of his Muslim colleagues in the Khilafat movement. Despite his several arrests and imprisonments by the British army, he formed the *Anjuman-i-Islah-ul-Afaghana* (the Society for the Reformation of Afghans) in April 1921 and later he instituted the first branch of *Azad Islamia Madrassa*. Ghaffar Khan's compassionate character and his empathetic method of practicing nonviolence convinced the Pashtoons that the only panacea for their blood feuds and factionalism was adoption of nonviolence and strict adherence to it. Truth, love, and service were the three main principles which gave shape to Ghaffar Khan's conception of a nonviolent public sphere. As such, a very important aspect of his thought and action was to bring about an inter-faith dialogue between the Hindus and Muslims, while condemning the communal politics of the Muslim League or the Hindutva. As a Muslim voice of nonviolence, Ghaffar Khan was revered by Mahatma Gandhi, who viewed Khan and his Pathan Red Shirts as an illustration of the moral courage and compassionate citizenry it takes to live a nonviolent life. As for Badshah Khan,

> from Gandhi, he took not only the creed of non-violence but also a whole way of life; one cannot, for example, think of Maulana Azad or Jinnah going to live in the sweepers' colony of the Valmikis in Delhi, as Ghaffar Khan repeatedly did, in Gandhi's company. And yet, his almost mythical stature among the Pathans he owed entirely to his own work, and not an iota of it to his colleagues in the Indian National Congress.[6]

To Ghaffar Khan, a Pashtun in particular, and a Muslim in general, was the one who knew how to practice compassionate understanding in regard to the Other, even the worst enemy. That is why, he called on God and on Gandhi's nonviolence as a strategy of dialogical resistance. As such, Ghaffar Khan's movement was much more than an army of nonviolent Pashtuns. Through the work of the *Khudai Khidmatgar*, Ghaffar Khan aimed at a revolution of values of the Pashtun society. He wanted to empower the Pashtuns in the same way that Gandhi empowered women and the Untouchables in India, in helping them to take charge of their destiny through self-realization and self-governance. "The basic principles of Khan's philosophy rested on nonviolence and self-restraint as well as reform at the social, political and economic levels. Service to humanity, truth, purity and struggle were at

74   *Comparative Approaches to Compassion*

its core."[7] Accordingly, despite his belief in secularism, Ghaffar Khan was very close to Gandhian vision of spiritualization and ethicization of politics.

> An examination of his philosophy shows that he firmly believed in the superiority of religion as a guide to practical living over the norms of cultural practice. Khan's greatest achievement was in fostering a philosophy of non-violence in a society that takes pride in having guns in their hands. Instead of looking to guns or other weapons as a source of pride, Khan upheld religion as a source of pride, as well as forgiveness and patience as virtues.[8]

Undoubtedly, Ghaffar Khan was in full harmony with his principles of unconditional compassion and empathy for humanity. To be sure, his exemplarity as a political leader and a social reformer was completed by his Sufi type values as a Muslim. Comparing Ghaffar Khan with Mahatma Gandhi, a contemporary biographer of his had the following opinion:

> If Ghaffar Khan has arrived at the philosophy of nonviolence, it is absolutely no wonder. Of the two, Ghaffar Khan and Mahatma Gandhi, my personal view is that the former has achieved a higher level of spirituality. The Khan has reached heaven, while the Pandit is firmly on the earth but ironically enough, the Mahatma is struggling in the air! Ghaffar Khan, like Shelley, has come from heaven to the earth, while Mahatma Gandhi, like Keats, is going from earth to the heaven. Hence, I do not understand why Ghaffar Khan should be called the Frontier Gandhi. There is no other reason except this that the Mahatma was earlier in the field, more ambitious than spiritual, and has been able to capture, somehow or the other, a greater publicity. If we judge a person by spiritual qualities, Mahatma Gandhi should rather be called the Indian Khan than Ghaffar Khan the Frontier Gandhi: true, there the matter ends.[9]

It is true that India's independence was not achieved purely through the sole efforts of Mahatma Gandhi. But one should also not forget that leaders of the Indian independence like Nehru, Azad, Patel, and Ghaffar Khan and humanity in general owe their knowledge of *Satyagraha* and the success of nonviolence in the process of India's anti-colonial struggle to Gandhi. It is a fact that without Gandhi Abdul Ghaffar Khan or any other compassionate and humanist player of the history of twentieth century would not have succeeded in turning *ahimsa* into a strong moral alternative for the future of humanity. Consequently, Khan Abdul Ghaffar Khan was among the very few who understood Gandhi's message of nonviolence and supported him until the end. As such, all his life, he remained faithful to Gandhi's words and deeds. He also had a fair idea of Gandhi's politics of compassion and his own devotion to a peaceful and tolerant Islam, and the unique way of knowing how to turn these two testaments into a moral capital. Therefore, far from considering nonviolence uniquely as an instrument of national liberation, Ghaffar Khan followed the path of Gandhi by turning Gandhian nonviolence and ethics of empathy into a process of coming to maturity of the Indian self. He was well aware of his task when he affirmed in 1985,

> Today's world is traveling in some strange direction. You see that the world is going toward destruction and violence. And the specialty of violence is to create hatred and fear among people. I am a believer in nonviolence and I say that no peace or tranquility will descend upon the world until nonviolence is practiced, because nonviolence is love and it stirs courage in people. There is advantage only in construction. I want to tell you categorically I will not support anybody in destruction.[10]

Nowhere does Gandhi's compassionate interdependence, empathetic citizenry, and ethics of nonviolence emerge in such a poignant manner as in the figure and action of Martin Luther King, Jr. Martin discovered Gandhi before he began to become Dr. King in a country where, in the words of James Baldwin, "Negroes... [were] taught really to despise themselves from the moment their eyes open on the world. "[11] As King explains in his *Autobiography*, the first time he heard of Gandhi was at a lecture by Dr. Mordecai Johnson, president of Howard University. Gandhi's message of nonviolence opened a new spiritual horizon to the young Martin. Gandhi, thus, became a significant source of inspiration to King, who found in the philosophy of nonviolence a more practical and pragmatic version of the teachings of Jesus Christ in his *Sermon on the Mount*. King dedicated himself to the Gandhian idea of *Satyagraha* as a philosophy of praxis. As a result, with the Montgomery Bus Boycott in 1955, he realized that the Gandhian *Satyagraha* was the best method of nonviolent emancipation and inclusive reconciliation which could realize the Christian principles of love and compassion. According to King, Gandhi "was probably the first person in history to lift the love ethic of Jesus above mere interaction between individuals to a powerful effective social force on a large scale."[12] However, King needed a period of intellectual incubation to be able to put the *Gospel* of Jesus and Gandhi's *Satyagraha* together. It took him some time to understand the moral power of compassion next to the vast socio-political potentiality of Gandhian nonviolence. According to Marshall Frady, Martin Luther King, Jr.'s biographer, "As the confrontation in Montgomery wore on far beyond King's original suppositions, it was as if he sensed himself being gradually enfolded into some wider embrace of fate. He declared, 'We are caught in a great moment of history-it is bigger than Montgomery.'" And like an untried actor suddenly finding himself cast in a far greater play than he'd ever reckoned on, he began flexing his potential, testing his arts over the course of his messages through the following months, his full vision emerging only through that long succession of mass meeting exhortations. Those exhortations had already begun prompting speculations among some that he could just turn out the American Gandhi, but he still had only a summary familiarity with Gandhi's ideas and meaning. While rapidly applying himself to learning more about this figure increasingly cited now as his possible antecedent, he yet averred later, "This business of passive resistance and nonviolence is the *gospel* of Jesus. I went to Gandhi through Jesus."[13] One can make here a comparison between King and Ghaffar Khan. As Ghaffar Khan came to Gandhi through his "soft reading" of Islam, so did King, through his emancipative theology and an original African-American interpretation of the message of Christ. In that sense, Martin Luther King, Jr.'s moral saga of nonviolence was that of a creative conscience inclined toward love and justice.

The Kingian dynamic of empathetic justice found its moral foundation in the Christian notion of *Agape* love. While distinguishing between three different Greek words for love: *Eros*, *Philia*, and *Agape*, King argued that Agape was the only way of love which could confront the evil and not the evildoer. As a matter of fact, he referred to *Agape* as a self-less and disinterested love, in contradistinction to *Eros* as romantic love and *Philia* as friendly love. Following the teachings of Jesus of Nazareth and his Apostles, King believed that only *Agape* love was the true path to realize and practise compassion in relation to the Other. The originality of King, as a Baptist minister and a follower of Mahatma Gandhi, was his moral commitment to compassion and nonviolence in the making of a loving community against a society of racial and social injustice. This Kingian moral attitude and political vision also illustrated the fact that the journey in the direction of the realization of compassion was a struggle for justice and toward a revolution of values. As Dr. King underlined:

> A true revolution of values will soon cause us to question the fairness and justice of many of our past and present policies. On the one hand we are called to play the good Samaritan on life's roadside; but that will be only an initial act. One day we must come to see that the whole Jericho road must be transformed so that men and women will not be constantly beaten and robbed as they make their journey on life's highway. True compassion is more than flinging a coin to a beggar; it is not haphazard and superficial. It comes to see that an edifice which produces beggars needs restructuring.[14]

For King, there was no such thing as true justice without love. In the same way, he observed that the injustice of the oppressors should always be met with a forgiving love. As such, King considered justice as an *agapic* activity which contributed to the sustainability of the Beloved Community. King conceived the Beloved Community beyond the American society and in terms of a cosmic fellowship which would include all races and all nations. This is because, for King, compassion constituted plurality. It involved, therefore, interdependence and global responsibility. This recognition of human solidarity constituted the essence of the Beloved Community. Ultimately, for King, the Beloved Community was plural and it involved a deep moral and spiritual transformation of social, economic, and political values.

Thus, it would seem to follow from King's own perspective that if the realization of community requires the transcendence of racism, it must also entail the transcendence of the system of economic exploitation that gave birth to racism. In short, community requires the transcendence of capitalism and its alienations. King's critique of capitalism, which some writers think begins only post-Selma, actually precedes Montgomery, and proceeds from the same moral principles as does the critique of racism.... But after Selma there does seem to be an increasing emphasis on themes of poverty and exploitation, on militarism and imperialism—and on the interrelation of these with each other and with racism. And in his critique of these social evils the concern is always for a community of freedom, and underlying values of dignity, freedom and human solidarity.[15]

Thus, King was not only trying to save the soul of the American society, but also struggling to redefine and re-structure humanity in terms of a new existential and moral approach. In his messianic vision, the racial crisis in America was linked to all elements of colonial and imperialistic injustices around the world. In the manner of Jesus and Gandhi, King saw radical compassion as a way of moral and social struggle for those who were oppressed, humiliated, and de-humanized. In the words of Cornel West,

The radical King was first and foremost a revolutionary Christian- a black Baptist minister and pastor whose intellectual genius and rhetorical power was deployed in the name of the Gospel of Jesus Christ. King understood this good news to be primarily radical love in freedom and radical freedom in love, a fallible enactment of the Beloved Community or finite embodiment of the Kingdom of God... King's radical love was

Christocentric in content and black in character... The black character of King's radical love was its roots in the indescribable terror and inimitable trauma of being black in white supremacist America, during slavery, Jim Crow, Sr., or Jim Crowe, Jr.[16]

King viewed compassionate interdependence as a participation in the loving and forgiving capacities of Jesus. But, by following Gandhi, he was also aware of the fact that nonviolence is a creative direct action, which helps individuals and communities to confront injustices and inequalities. By incorporating compassion and nonviolence into his conception of *Agape* love, King appealed to the centrality of self-suffering as a righteous path to restore a broken community and to serve humanity. That is why, King considered each one of his nonviolent campaigns as a challenge to the injustice of the White community and a re-examination of the power of compassion and endurance in suffering of the African-Americans. This dynamic of surfacing challenges and assumptions was, therefore, much bigger than the time and place of the confrontation. For example, in relation with the Montgomery Bus Boycott, King underlined:

The basic conflict is not really over the buses. Yet we believe that, if the method we use in dealing with equality in the buses can eliminate injustice within ourselves, we shall at the same time be attacking the basis of injustice-man's hostility to man. This can only be done when we challenge the white community to re-examine its assumptions as we are now prepared to re-examine ours.[17]

As a moral leader and a follower of Jesus and Gandhi, King was someone who knew how to bear the cross and die on it. This was for him the best way to practise what he called "a cosmic companionship" and to overcome the tyranny of violence and

The Twin Heritage of Gandhian Nonviolence 81

hatred. For King, the test of compassionate self-suffering was also a way to show that the oppressed was "the truly civilized party."[18] He, therefore, did not envision compassion for the Other as a random act. Following Gandhi, King was convinced that one could conquer the hearts and minds of the enemies through nonviolent action. Referring to the Mahatma as a conqueror, he affirmed:

> This little man, one of the greatest conquerors that the world has ever known. Somebody said that when Mahatma Gandhi was coming over to England for the roundtable conference in 1932, a group of people stood there waiting. And somebody pointed out, and while they were waiting somebody said, 'You see around that cliff? That was where Julius Caesar came, the way he came in when he invaded Britain years ago.' And then somebody pointed over to another place and said, 'That was the way William the Conqueror came in. They invaded years ago in the Battle of Hastings.' Then somebody else looked over and said, 'There is another conqueror coming in. In just a few minutes the third and greatest conqueror that has ever come into Great Britain.' And strangely enough, this little man came in with no armies, no guards around him, no military might, no beautiful clothes, just loin cloth, but this man proved to be the greatest conqueror that the British Empire ever faced. He was able to achieve, through love and nonviolence, the independence of his people and break the backbone of the British Empire. 'Ye shall do greater works than I have done.' And this is exemplified in the life of Mahatma Gandhi.[19]

What King admired in Gandhi was not only his tender-heartedness in the act of empathy and compassion, but also his toughmindedness when it came to be an anti-conformist dissenter. Consequently, King saw a *satyagrahi* as a kind and

82 *Comparative Approaches to Compassion*

gentle but toughminded person. In one of his sermons on the subject he argued:

> There are hardhearted and bitter individuals among us who would combat the opponent with physical violence and corroding hatred... There is a third way open to us in our quest for freedom, namely, non-violent resistance, that combines toughmindedness and tender-heartedness and avoids the complacency and do-nothingness of the softminded and the violence and bitterness of the hardhearted... Through nonviolent resistance we shall be able to rise to oppose the unjust system and at the same time love the perpetrators of the system.[20]

It goes without saying that for Martin Luther King, Jr. love and compassion are community-oriented concepts. Accordingly, suffering, because of the injustice committed by the Other, was considered by King as an empathetic ability to identify with the redemptive power of the *Agape* love, rather than being an act which takes pride in being kind and just. That is why, King identified "only *Agape* as love relevant beyond friendship and intimate relationships to the political practice of nonviolence, and to the social, cultural, and political conditions of nations. *Agape* goes public; *Philia* and *Eros* remain disassociated from public affairs."[21] Consequently, King followed Gandhi in the process of politicizing love and compassion. As such, he looked for a compassionate and empathetic agency in the nonviolent confrontation with the hatred and violence of the Other. King certainly regarded Gandhian *Satyagraha* as the best and most pragmatic way of putting Jesus's love ethic into action, but he was also looking for a creative strategy to build a coalition of souls, in order to project compassion and empathy to the center of what he called "the world house." To be sure, rather than simply accepting that the only responses to poverty was Christian charity, King reminded his fellow Americans and others around the world that poverty is unjust, unnecessary and outright evil. Once again, King put Christian compassion as a dissenting agency and Gandhian nonviolent direct action back-to-back, by trying "to enable everybody to understand that we are clothed in a single garment of destiny, and whatever affects one nation directly in the world, indirectly affects all."[22] King understood that there was no way to attain a universal harmony among human communities without getting involved with the miseries and sufferings of other individuals and nations. That is why he was concerned with the gospel of peace in his writings and actions. For him, as it was the case for Gandhi, the world stood on the brink of annihilation for not choosing the way of nonviolence. He wrote:

> In a world facing the revolt of ragged and hungry masses of God's children; in a world torn between the tensions of East and West, white and colored, individuals and collectivists; in a world whose cultural and spiritual power lags so far behind her technological capabilities that we live each day on the verge of nuclear co-annihilation; in this world, nonviolence is no longer an option for intellectual analysis, it is an imperative for action.[23]

Driven by the belief that compassion was the power which would enable God's one family to shape its understanding of justice, King renewed the Christian message of the redemptive good-will of love. Subsequently, for Martin Luther King, Jr., the struggle for fairness and righteousness was a great effort to establish human interrelatedness and cosmic friendship. As a matter of fact, King knew well that "God is not interested merely in the freedom of black men, brown men, and yellow men; God is interested in

84   *Comparative Approaches to Compassion*

the freedom of the whole human race."[24] Throughout his life, Dr. King's Christian vision and his faith in Gandhian nonviolence had assured him that compassion and love are moral demands of life. He, therefore, reminded the Blacks and the Whites in America that segregation as morally and politically wrong and against the just nature of the universe. Accordingly, King considered the struggle against racism as a way of looking at a social evil through the lens of Gandhian nonviolence. That is why, the Gandhian philosophy of nonviolence became a guiding light in King's campaigns for civil rights and social justice in America. Thus, he affirmed:

> The experience in Montgomery did more to clarify my thinking on the question of nonviolence than all of the books that I had read. As the days unfolded I became more and more convinced of the power of nonviolence. Living through the actual experience of the protest, nonviolence became more than a method to which I gave intellectual assent; it became a commitment to a way of life. Many issues I had not cleared up intellectually concerning nonviolence were now solved in the sphere of practical action.[25]

And with his having followed his original experience up to the last day of his life on April 4, 1968, he made us understand that the philosophy of nonviolence is a weapon of the compassionate and a power of love and justice which serves humanity. According to Marshall Frady, "in one of his last addresses to his congregation at Ebenezer, [King] declared that all he wanted said about him when he died was for somebody to mention that day that "Martin Luther King, Jr., tried to give his life serving others... .that [he] tried to love and serve humanity."[26]

5

Toward a Compassionate Civilization: From *Swaraj* to *The Beloved Community*

Nearly sixty years ago, Martin Luther King, Jr. wrote the following words, to be handed down the generations: "Man was born into barbarism when killing his fellow man was a normal condition of existence. He became endowed with a conscience. And he has now reached the day when violence toward another human being must become as abhorrent as eating another's flesh."[1] King recognized the danger of violence for the future of our human civilization. But, at the same time, he took the opportunity to show us the possibility of nonviolence as a civilizational dynamic transcending our pessimism and despair. King, in the same way as Gandhi and Khan Abdul Ghaffar Khan, knew that if the banner of nonviolence is lowered, inequalities and injustices will not be exposed and challenged. As Dr. King put it, "Freedom is not won by a passive acceptance of suffering. Freedom is won by a struggle against suffering... No great victories are won in a war for the transformation of a whole people without total participation. Less than this will not create a new society."[2] King was well aware of the fact that the main problem was not only racism and fanaticism, but also the conformist and complacent attitude of citizens who preferred to be armed chair spectators of the tragedies of the world. He, therefore, argued: "Let us be those creative dissenters who will call our beloved nation to a higher destiny, to a new plateau of compassion, to a more noble expression of humanness."[3] For King,

86   *Comparative Approaches to Compassion*

the question on the agenda had two sides: how to think in terms of a compassionate civilization? and how to give a new breadth of meaning to nonviolent dissent?

Unsurprisingly, the two questions raised by Martin Luther King, Jr. were the same asked by Mahatma Gandhi in 1909 his seminal book, *Hind Swaraj*. Gandhi explained the purpose of writing such a book. As he underlined, *Hind Swaraj*,

> was written in 1908 during my return voyage from London to South Africa in answer to the Indian school of violence and its prototype in South Africa. I came in contact with every known Indian anarchist in London. Their bravery impressed me, but I felt that their zeal was misguided. I felt that violence was no remedy for India's ills, and that her civilization required the use of a different and higher weapon for self-protection. The *Satyagraha* of South Africa was still an infant hardly two years old. But it had developed sufficiently to permit me to write of it with some degree of confidence. What I wrote was so much appreciated that it was published as a booklet. It attracted some attention in India. The Bombay Government prohibited its circulation. I replied by publishing its translation. I thought it was due to my English friends that they should know its contents.[4]

Actually, by writing *Hind Swaraj*, Gandhi was trying to respond critically to two challenges at the same time: on the one hand, to confront the violent ideas and project of the Indian anarchists; on the other, emphasizing on the immoral nature of modern civilization, while trying to redefine the principal purpose of a civilization. Accordingly, Gandhi suggested his own definition of the concept of civilization as "that mode of conduct that points out to man the path of duty."[5] Of course, it goes without saying that for Gandhi, duty and morality went hand in hand.

Gandhi was, therefore, appealing to a moral civilization which was well aware of its deeds and actions. What Gandhi criticized and rejected in modern civilization was its inability to be self-conscious and to enhance virtues which could help human beings to emancipate themselves spiritually and politically. Gandhi considered modern civilization as a world that ignored itself. As Tridip Suhrud points out correctly:

> For Gandhi, the essential character of modern civilization is not represented by either the Empire, or the speed of railways, the contractual nature of society brought about by Western law, nor by the vivisection practised in modern medicine. It is also not represented by use of violence as a legitimate means of expressing political dissent and obtaining political goals, even though these are significant markers of modern civilization. The essential character of modern civilization is represented by denial of a fundamental possibility, that of knowing oneself.[6]

Gandhi's Socratic approach to the concept of civilization provided him with the importance of self-realization as a central theme of Indian nationalism. Gandhi's critique of modern civilization in *Hind Swaraj* is one of the greatest Socratic gestures of intellectual self-examination in the history of modern thought. It is all the more necessary to point out that Gandhi's critical attitude was an effort in asking the right questions at the right time about the obstacles to the self-understanding of modern civilization. What Gandhi called "civilization" was actually a spiritual mode of conduct, which should appeal to the conscience of humanity. Therefore, Gandhi explicitly assumed a fundamental moral distinction between a civilization of nonviolence crystalized in the act of compassion and empathy, and the self-destructive modern civilization represented by colonialism, materialism, and capitalism. Hence, Gandhi's project of civilization was to liberate humankind from the restraints and alienation of an unethical and violent civilization, which subverted and destroyed traditional modes of thinking and living. As such, we can say that *Hind Swaraj* is a manifesto of spiritual emancipation that suggests the quest for Truth, in opposition to a self-centered and egoistic mode of living. Therefore, Gandhi introduced his readers to the question of means and ends and a realistic balance between the two. For Gandhi, violence was "linked to modern civilization." It had to be avoided "not only because *ahimsa* (nonviolence, love) is superior to morality, but also because violence creates a distance between the self and the pursuit of Truth... Violence for Gandhi[made] the possibility of knowing oneself even fainter. He, therefore, [decried] the argument that the end justifies the means... Gandhi [argued] for purity of both the means and the end."[7]

In his experiential quest for Truth, Gandhi stressed the importance of reaching a nonviolent society based on compassion. Compassion was described as the means to realize Truth and nonviolence. However, Gandhi was convinced that searching for Truth would help people to be more compassionate and tolerant. This would seem to be substantiated by Gandhi's argument: "I would say 'means are after all everything'. As the means so the end. There is no wall of separation between means and end... Realization of the goal is in exact proportion to that of the means."[8] Obviously, by reading Gandhi we realize that he put a great deal of stress on the relation between Truth and civilization. For him, a compassionate civilization, which was defined by the recognition of the otherness of the Other could not be untruthful. Undoubtedly, the essence of Gandhi's idea of a compassionate civilization is the empathetic unity of the self and the other. He did not consider the civilizing process as a mechanical movement toward progress. Civilization, for Gandhi, required the promotion of the spirit of mutuality, solidarity, and interdependence. In his task to defend a compassionate civilization, Gandhi invited individuals to rule themselves against their weaker natures by becoming self-governing agents. The basic idea of a moral and compassionate that Gandhi provided in *Hind Swaraj* remained a constant reference in his later social and political speeches and writings. For Gandhi, civilization was a moral and spiritual task, not an idea taken for granted and used as a justification to commit barbaric acts of colonialism and imperialism. As such, Gandhi's civilizational approach to a change of heart and values in Indian society and beyond emerged essentially as a mode of social interconnectedness based on the empowerment of every citizen, and as a common horizon of humanity, which strengthened the process of thinking about the otherness of the Other. By addressing the question of the otherness of the Other from a civilizational point of view, Gandhi was trying to cultivate the individual's capacity for ethical citizenship and empathetic mutuality. Subsequently, from Gandhi's perspective, nonviolence encouraged an awareness, which moved the individual away from a utilitarian egocentricity and closer to a compassionate shared suffering. What is so fascinating and relevant with the Gandhian civilizational approach to compassion and empathy is that Gandhi understood it as a process of freedom-making and self-governing, which should also include the Other as the Other. Moreover, in the eyes of Gandhi, the civilizational pursuit of Truth should contribute to the anti-colonial and democratic construction of *Swaraj* as a political ideal. Therefore, dwelling on the nature of *Swaraj*, Gandhi argued in *Hind Swaraj*:

90   *Comparative Approaches to Compassion*

It is *Swaraj* when we learn to rule ourselves. It is, therefore, in the palm of our hands. Do not consider this *Swaraj* to be like a dream. There is no idea of sitting still. The *Swaraj* that I wish to picture is such that, after we have once realized it, we shall endeavour to the end of our life-time to persuade others to do likewise. But such *Swaraj* has to be experienced, by each one for himself. One drowning man will never save another. Slaves ourselves, it would be a mere pretension to think of freeing others.[9]

Undoubtedly, *Swaraj* was the mother concept of Gandhi's thinking on compassionate civilization and nonviolence. Truly, Gandhi, unlike Jawaharlal Nehru and Sardar Patel, was more concerned with *Hind Swaraj*, than with only India's independence. For him, *Swaraj* was a matter of self-respect, self-realization, and self-government. In response to a correspondent on October 20, 1929, Gandhi underlined:

The writer has narrowed down the very meaning of *swaraj* itself. The gentleman seems to believe that swaraj means the transfer of power from British hands to Indian hands. To my mind *swaraj* means regulated power in the hands of thirty crores of people. Where there is such rule, even a young girl will feel safe and, if the imagination of a poet is correct, animals like dogs, etc. who live among human beings will have a similar feeling of safety. We shall have to arrive at various basic decisions in regard to *swaraj*, because under *swaraj* such decisions are not subject to officials in power but are based on truth and justice. I have succinctly called this kin of *swaraj Ramarajya*.[10]

Therefore, as Gandhi understood, *Swaraj* was not only a political ideal, but also an ethical value. That is why it included both the public and the private spheres. In other words, from Gandhi's point of view, building a self-governed society demanded self-disciplined and self-regulated individuals. However, Gandhi was fully conscious that being autonomous meant recognizing the autonomy of the Other. As such, Gandhi was not thinking in terms of the State, but in relation with civil society, which included the Self and the Other. He emphasized on a new model of human interconnectedness, a non-utilitarian and compassionate civilization, which could take humanity to a higher moral level. For Gandhi, civilization has to give primacy to moral progress of humanity, rather than just generate tendencies toward meaninglessness, complacency, and violence. Gandhi was convinced that civilization should help humanity realize the path of compassion and nonviolence, by putting morality before materialism. That is why for him, *Swaraj* was a selfless and compassionate concept. To Gandhi, *Swaraj* meant, self-respect and dignity for the poorest of all Indians. Gandhi was well aware of the importance of pluralism of ideas and values because of the dissimilarities and differences that existed in Indian society. Consequently, he discussed compassion and equality next to each other. Thus, Gandhi criticized the bureaucratic and dominative essence of modernity, while trying to replace its monolithic and positivistic vision of reality with a dialogical and intercultural outlook. Accordingly, the Gandhian idea of *Swaraj*, as a compassionate civilization, was based on a new form of solidarity—that of shared humanity. Thus, Gandhi was rightly worried about the future of Indian society as a nation which would accept modern values with no critical distancing. Characterizing *Swaraj* in its innovative and multidimensional essence, Gandhi remained hopeful about the power of nonviolence in correcting all errors of modernity. In response to his critics, he affirmed the following in 1931: "Of course, you will say that India free can become a menace herself. But let us assume she will behave herself

92   Comparative Approaches to Compassion

with her doctrine of nonviolence if she achieves her freedom through it, and for all her bitter experience of being a victim of exploitation."[11] As a result, we understand well why Gandhi was against a "Hindu Raj" or a "Muslim Raj." According to him, *Swaraj* had a multi-religious and intercultural essence. In other words, Gandhi considered *Swaraj* as an interconnected principle and an interrelated ideal. For him, *Swaraj* was a compassionate mode of thinking and acting for the survival of the otherness of the Other. Last, but not least, Gandhi considered *Swaraj* as "the constantly confirmed consciousness of being in charge of one's destiny, not just about liberty but about power."[12]

From what has been said hitherto, it can be deduced that Gandhi regarded the compassionate civilization as a self-transformative and self-governing entity, which could be attained only by means of Truth and nonviolence. It is clear then that Gandhi's social and political thought had an ethical foundation which found its full self-expression in the idea of compassionate understanding and empathetic inclusiveness. That is why Gandhi believed that nonviolence and the quest for Truth required a loving soul in service of humanity. As such, Gandhi envisioned the compassionate civilization as a civilization of love and forgiveness, not that of hatred and revenge. And yet, he referred to love as a form of struggle and not passivity. He said:

> Love can fight; often, it is obliged to. In the intoxication of power, man fails to see his error. When that happens, a Satyagrahi does not sit still. He suffers. He disobeys the ruler's orders and his laws in a civil manner, and willingly submits to the penalties of such disobedience, for instance, imprisonment and gallows. Thus is the soul disciplined. In this, one never finds that one's time has been wasted and, if it is subsequently realized that

Toward a Compassionate Civilization 93

such respectful disobedience was an error, the consequences are suffered merely by the Satyagrahi and his co-workers. In the event, no bitterness develops between the Satyagrahi and those in power; the latter, on the contrary, willingly yield to him. They discover that they cannot command the Satyagrahi's obedience. They cannot make him do anything against his will. And this is the consummation of *Swaraj*, because it means complete independence. It need not be assumed that such resistance is possible only against civilized rulers. Even a heart of flint will melt in the fire kindled by the power of the soul. Even a Nero becomes a lamb when he faces love. This is no exaggeration. It is as true as an algebraic equation. This Satyagrahi is India's distinctive weapon. It has had others but *Satyagraha* has been in greater use. It is an unfailing source of strength, and is capable of being used at all times and under all circumstances. It requires no stamp of approval from the Congress or any other body. He who knows its power cannot but use it. Even as the eyelashes automatically protect the eyes, so does *Satyagraha*, when kindled, automatically protect the freedom of the soul.[13]

On reflection, we can say that Gandhi referred to compassion and nonviolence as his eternal creed and the law of the human race. As a matter of fact, what he suggested to humanity in general was a civilization, which unlike the one we live in, would care for all living beings. As a result, Gandhi had no doubt that nonviolent methods could bring such a compassionate civilization about. Therefore, a satyagrahi did not "wish for destruction of his antagonist, he [did] not vent anger on him; but [had]only compassion for him."[14] In other words, Gandhi regarded nonviolence as the only gateway to a compassionate civilization.

Martin Luther King, Jr. sympathized with Gandhi's idea of a compassionate civilization and approved of the nonviolent struggle for it. Actually, more than any other moral leader in the

94   *Comparative Approaches to Compassion*

past seventy-five years, King understood that humankind needs to redefine its civilizational purposes for a better future, inspired by global responsibility and respect of life. King wanted to be remembered after his death as a drum major, but he added,

> If you want to say that I was a drum major, say that I was a drum major for justice. Say that I was a drum major for peace. I was a drum major for righteousness. And all of the other shallow things will not matter. I won't have any money to leave behind. I won't have the fine and luxurious things of life to leave behind. But I just want to leave a committed life behind. And that's all I want to say.[15]

All his life, King sided with the poor, the oppressed, the downtrodden. His struggle was not only against the white supremacy, but also against all those in America and around the world who believed that hatred and murder were solutions to social and economic problems. In a sense, for King, dissent was a high form of compassion. Compassion was a mode of being and a manner of thinking which sat at the center of King's social and political thought. Accordingly, King saw compassion as a nonviolent struggle which could empower the unfree Blacks in America and teach the Whites to respect and join this fight for freedom. As Cornel West argues, "King's radical love of an often unloved people – black people – is the basis of his much-heralded love of white people. His radical love is inseparable from the radical freedom he wants for an unfree people – and for all others."[16] King was quite aware of the fact that with compassion came self-respect and sense of dignity, followed by the courage to stand up and protest against injustice. Hence, in King's view, compassion for the otherness of the Other called upon individuals of strong conviction and social responsibility, rather than conformists and complacent characters. Jesus's disavowal of revenge and violence guided King toward the total rejection of the ethic of retaliation and acceptance of compassion as a mode of dissent. Jesus's command to love was comprehended by King as a creative force, making the way toward the beauty of God and the good in the world. Jesus's imperative of love and compassion showed King how to bridge the gap between what is and what ought to be. As a result, King came to see his struggle for a compassionate civilization as a profound existential and ethical matter. And so, as a result of this, the work of compassion in history, as an unarmed truth, became the way of Black emancipation in particular and a nonviolent world in general. By instituting compassion in the public sphere, King revived and resuscitated Gandhi's message of *Hind Swaraj*. Gandhi saw in his ideal of *Swaraj*, the power of self-affirmation and self-governance of Indians. Correspondingly, King's appeal to African-Americans was to assert their will to dignity and honor, and to underline their contribution in democratizing American democracy. As King proclaimed:

> The Negro will only be free when he reaches down to the inner depths of his own being and signs with the pen and ink of assertive manhood his own emancipation proclamation. With a spirit straining toward true self-esteem, the Negro must boldly throw off the manacles of self-abnegation and say to himself and to the world, "I am somebody. I am a person. I am a man with dignity and honor. I have a rich and noble history, however painful and exploited that history has been. I am black and comely." This self-affirmation is the black man's need, made compelling by the white man's crimes against him. This is positive and necessary power for black people.[17]

King considered the Beloved Community as the logical and inevitable outcome of the synthesis of Jesus's philosophy of compassion and the Gandhian strategy of nonviolence. As such, he came to understand the struggle for compassionate justice and social equality as part of the process of self-examination of human civilization. King understood well that the making of a compassionate civilization demanded an effort of self-transformation and spiritual emancipation. King's vision of a Beloved Community was that of an inclusive brotherhood with a sense of responsibility. In other words, he believed that recognition of one's indebtedness and one's responsibility to others would lead to a community of reconciliation and interdependence. Ultimately, this was also King's vision of democracy, which he saw as a compassionate, just, and inclusive regime. In the same breath, he believed that war in Vietnam was getting involved in injustice and evil abroad. King considered the American foreign policy as "arrogant" and against such arrogance he suggested the two imperatives of justice and compassion. King believed that the decision had to be made: either war in Vietnam or war on poverty in the United States. Maybe that is why King called war in Vietnam "a far deeper malady within the American spirit."[18] King criticized the United States for being on the wrong side of the revolution against poverty and exploitation. He believed that a civilization run by warmongers and greedy capitalists is a broken civilization with no future. That is because individual dignity and Beloved Community were inseparable in the mind of Dr. King. At all times and in all places, the self was related to the other. "We are made to live together," King underlined, "because of the interrelated structure of reality."[19] As such, from the perspective of Martin Luther King, Jr. the conception and realization of

Toward a Compassionate Civilization

a Beloved Community involved a deep moral and spiritual transformation of the individuals and communities. The Beloved Community, as King understood it, involved political and social relationships created by compassion. In final analysis, King's view of the Beloved Community was very similar to Mahatma Gandhi's idea of "spiritualization of politics." In a speech on May 1915 at Government High School in Bangalore, Gandhi argued:

> What is the meaning of spiritualising the political life of the country? What is the meaning of spiritualising myself? That question has come before me often and often and to you it may seem one thing, to me it may seem another thing; it may mean different things to the different members of the Servants of India Society itself. It shows much difficulty and it shows the difficulties of all those who want to love their country, who want to serve their country and who want to honour their country. I think the political life must be an echo of private life and that there cannot be any divorce between the two. I was by the side of that saintly politician[Gokhale] to the end of his life and I found no ego in him. I ask you members of the Social Service League, if there is no ego in you. If he wanted to shine, he wanted to shine in the political field of his country, he did so not in order that he might gain public applause, but in order that his country may gain. He developed every particular faculty in him, not in order to win the praise of the world for himself but in order that his country may gain. He did not seek public applause, but they were showered upon him, they were thrust upon him; he wanted that his country may gain and that was his great inspiration.[20]

Assuredly, both Gandhi and King understood that to attain a compassionate civilization humanity needed to excel. Thus, as Socratic dissidents, both Gandhi and King knew well that excellence was an exemplary act, which was based on a public act of questioning. In a Socratic manner, but in their own ways, Gandhi and King had examined lives. Their examined lives were means and ends based on nonviolence. But Gandhi and King also put into question the truths and beliefs that were at the foundation of modern life. Therefore, as dissident minds, they brought about a revaluation of the values of their Zeitgeist. There was, in sum, a general agreement between their moral commitment to the ideas of compassion and love and a clear commitment to nonviolent struggle against injustice. It is by referring to a higher law that Gandhi and King put compassion and nonviolence above the power of States and masses. As such, they became the master thinkers of a revolution against conformism and complacency in modern times. As citizen-dissidents, Gandhi and King continued to teach nonviolent protesters that responsible and morally committed individuals should be present in the public space where dialogue and dissent can defeat fanaticism and violence. For them, the voice of conscience transcended that of the State. Therefore, they both presented us with a comprehensive vision of moral conscience as a pathway to self-rule and self-transformation. Here again, we can evaluate the broader contribution of Gandhi to the ideal of a compassionate civilization. Gandhi and King continue to remain our contemporaries, mainly because their dissident act of proclaiming a compassionate civilization continues to be different from our habitual ways of being present in the global public space. Surprisingly, those who are familiar with the lives and works of Mahatma Gandhi and Martin Luther King, Jr. know that the moral pursuit of a compassionate civilization is actually a moment of existential crisis for humanity. No doubt, it will help humanity to create moments of rethinking the ethical and the political in the shadow of the spiritual. Compassion and nonviolence are, therefore, crucial concepts, at a time when the two projects of critical thinking and democratic questioning have retreated in our world. This is certainly the time to change our values, priorities, and perspective if humanity is to survive mediocrity and meaninglessness. It is time for humanity to understand that the consequences of its actions will be disastrous and catastrophic. This is where compassion and nonviolence as community-building values must play an important role and are vital requirements for establishing a common humanity. This is our unique window of opportunity to save humanity from itself. Therefore, our choice is no longer between good and evil, but between a civilization of compassion and love or a world of greed and violence. Maybe we should listen once again to what Mahatma Gandhi had to say, in a letter to T. de Manziarly on March 21, 1928. Gandhi wrote: "I would just like to say that whilst I am a passionate devotee of simplicity in life, I have also discovered that it is worthless unless the echo of simplicity comes from within. The modern organized artificiality of so-called civilized life cannot have any accord with true simplicity of heart."[21] Seeking to provide an alternative vision to the arrogance of modernity, Gandhi and King aimed to interpret everyday pictures of the world with a new philosophical outlook in which the role of moral conscience was to give compassion and nonviolence a significant role in the making of reality. However, they were quite aware of the fact that transcending human fragility was a great challenge in the making of a compassionate civilization.

6

Nelson Mandela: Common Humanity and Ethics of Empathy

"To me nonviolence has come to represent a panacea for all the evils that surround my people," Khan Abdul Ghaffar Khan argued. "Therefore I am devoting all my energies toward the establishment of a society that would be based on its principles of truth and peace."[1] Undoubtedly, these words could have been said by Nelson Mandela. Madiba, as he was referred to by South Africans, was a passionate believer, but he did not make use of his Christian faith directly in the public space. Hence, his approach to the question of compassion was very different from that of Mahatma Gandhi. More than anything, Mandela was a strategist of compassion. However, his vision of a common humanity was very similar to the Gandhian approach to Truth and *ahimsa* beyond all racial and religious differences and to the Kingian concept of "World House" which was based on a "cosmic companionship." Mandela's political philosophy was built upon the idea of compassionate fellowship among human beings.

> Like Gandhi, Mandela from the beginning of his career as a politicized lawyer stood for, and stood up for, human dignity, thereby exposing the hypocrisy of the opposition, who tended to claim the moral high ground in this respect. Like Gandhi, too, Mandela deployed nonviolent strategies in order to achieve his political aims, though Gandhi did so more persistently, under less oppressive duress.[2]

It remains quite clear that Mandela was a moral leader, like Dr. King and Abdul Ghaffar Khan, and of course, like them, he was an architect of compassion. For Mandela, the work of compassionate fellowship was practiced through civic dialogue. "Mandela over the years found a way of converting his respect for the human dignity in each and every person into a political practice through dialogue: making cross-border conversation a culture-wide expectation, and a means of mapping common ground and mutual regard."[3] For Mandela, the politics of reconciliation in South Africa was a process of moral act of self-transformation of a nation and its choice of living a new national life through compassionate fellowship. By giving priority to the ethical over the political, Nelson Mandela restored the idea of compassion in South African society by always reminding his supporters and enemies about the otherness of the Other. "Mandela increasingly approached others not as members of a certain party or group, but as human beings first and foremost, as unpredictable, complicated, yet always ethical (or potentially ethical) agents. He became more interested in likeness than in difference; he focused on interaction, not distinction or separation."[4] As such, Mandela's strategy of compassion was mainly defined by the process of overcoming the spirit of hatred, division, and mistrust. This sense of respect for the otherness of the Other found its center of gravity in the Ubuntu philosophy. Ubuntu could be roughly translated as "human kindness." The Ubuntu philosophy says: "I am what I am because of who we all are." It's a powerful thinking which helped Mandela to rebuild South Africa in the direction of reconciliation and unity. The practice of Ubuntu helped him to support the concept that everyone is part of the whole, therefore, he or she should be fully respected and acknowledged. This was immediately reflected by the following words of Archbishop Desmond Tutu: "A person with Ubuntu is open and available to others, affirming of others, does not feel threatened that others are able and good, for he or she has a proper self-assurance that comes from knowing that he or she belongs in a greater whole and is diminished when others are humiliated or diminished, when others are tortured or oppressed."[5] Following the philosophy of Ubuntu, Mandela's strategic gaze at compassion was exemplified by the exercise of an epistemic humility and listening to and learning from others. He, therefore, defined South Africa as a "common home" to both white and black South Africans. Accordingly, what Mandela showed the world was that if a nation decided to have a space of togetherness and plurality, it needed to take its guns and its knives and throw them into the sea. Assuredly, Mandela's aim was not to replace a white dictatorship with a black one. His aim was a democratic South Africa, and for that, he believed that South Africans should not waste their energy and destroy their unity by fighting among themselves. But at the same time, for Mandela, the work of compassion was that of re-humanizing the oppressed and the excluded. Mandela was the first to insist that a journey back into South Africa's violent past should be taken. As the chairman of the newly established Truth and Reconciliation Commission in April 1996, Archbishop Tutu argued that "reconciliation [was] not about being cosy; it [was] not about pretending that things were other than they were. Reconciliation based on falsehood, or not facing up to reality, [was] not true reconciliation and [would] not last."[6]

In agreement with Archbishop Tutu, Mandela believed that the central element in the TRC's approach was the quest of truth in the dialogical encounter between the oppressors and the victims.

104   *Comparative Approaches to Compassion*

Correspondingly, both Tutu and Mandela insisted that truth should be coupled with forgiveness, while compassion becomes a lesson of history against crime and punishment. In that sense:

> Mandela fell back on the shared experience of pain and anxiety as facilitators of his politics, (... .), [his] first essential goal was to neutralize the hegemonic effect of racial categorization, and the most effective way he set about doing that was to target the exact human virtue that the categorization sought to block: compassion. Mandela realized that a simple empathic gesture, however symbolic, would allow people from different racial and ethnic backgrounds to begin to engage one another as human beings, no longer as objects frozen in categories.[7]

Mandela's compassionate methodology in the South African Truth and Reconciliation Commission showed clearly that he preferred to use the "Ubuntu paradigm" instead of the "Nuremberg paradigm." Indeed, Mandela's nonviolent moral consciousness translated into a politics of empathy, compassion, and forgiveness, which linked existentially the otherness of the Other with the art of nation-building. "Nelson Mandela realized full well that empathy and the achievements of the Truth and Reconciliation Commission in the transition period are transient. The issues of social and economic injustices have to be addressed. The successes of the Truth and Reconciliation Commission have only set the stage for more encompassing and far-reaching deliberations on how South Africans can live together."[8] The concept of "sharing together" developed by Mandela to define the political exercise was in this respect very rich. Therefore, compassionate politics was exercised as soon as enemies came together to talk about a common situation and decided to act together in order to change this situation. As such, Mandela's never-ending struggle to end Apartheid in South

Common Humanity and Ethics of Empathy 105

Africa required a return to the African philosophy of "Ubuntu." Ubuntu became the philosophy that guided compassionate fellowship and nonviolent change in South Africa.

> Ubuntu, a Xhosa and Zulu philosophy, derivative of the South African Buntu language, is considered to be a dispositional quality of human virtue based on connection, community, and mutual caring for each other. It is the belief that sharing a universal bond connects all of humanity. Sharing, as an embodied action, allows for recognition of others' uniqueness and differences, and supports the process to bring others along.[9]

Mandela's appeal to compassionate fellowship and empathetic citizenry in South Africa was not only an extension of the spirit of Ubuntu, but also deeply influenced by the transformative nonviolence of Mahatma Gandhi. However, we can find the Gandhian phases of Mandela's political career only in the early and late phases of his life.

> Taking a chronological view of his career across five decades, 1950 to 2000, we see Mandela tracing an ideological parabola away from his early Gandhist phase, toward a support for armed resistance, and then, at the last, turning back to nonviolent ideas of political negotiation and compromise... [Mandela] and the other more radical ANC members were always intensely pragmatic about the use of militancy. In many ways they had to be-MK [*Umkhonto we Sizwe*] was a notoriously ineffective guerrilla force. They were keenly aware, more than Gandhi perhaps allowed, that nonviolence historically operated in dialectical tandem with outbreaks of violence, or what they called armed propaganda-the presentation, at least, of a front of armed resistance. Rather than being a conclusive shift away from passive resistance, Mandela's move to armed struggle entailed a tacit recognition that noncooperation

106   *Comparative Approaches to Compassion*

could not thrive as a politics without the accompaniment of some form of militancy.[10]

It is interesting that even during the sabotage campaign of the ANC against the Apartheid regime in the early 1960s, Mandela underlined the fact that struggle against a dictatorship should not involve loss of lives and it should "keep bitterness at a minimum level." Of course, he could have foreseen that during his years in prison, the Spear of the Nation, referred to as MK, would embrace a doctrine committed to the violent overthrow of the Apartheid regime. However, his political evolution and his embracement of the Gandhian principles during his twenty-seven years of imprisonment, empowered him with a new strategy of dialogue and negotiation which ended his presidency in 1994 and with the Truth and Reconciliation Commissions headed by Archbishop Tutu. It is interesting that for a man like Mandela the battle for human dignity did not concern only the Black population of South Africa, but also the Whites. As he wrote in *Long Walk to Freedom*, "I knew that people expected me to harbor anger toward whites. But I had none. In prison, my anger toward whites decreased, but my hatred for the system grew. I wanted South Africa to see that I loved even my enemies while I hated the system that turned us against one another."[11]

Mandela was fully conscious about the profoundly compassionate nature of transformative nonviolence. As he said in a speech, at the opening of the Gandhi Hall in Lenasia, on September 1992:

Gandhi pledged 21 years of his life to the development of non-racialism and democracy in our country it is our duty to ensure that we not only remember his deeds but that we emulate and uphold them. A united, non-racial, non-sexist and democratic

Common Humanity and Ethics of Empathy 107

South Africa will become the jewel of this planet. We face a bright future not withstanding the horrors of apartheid and its violence. We are dedicated to a negotiated settlement and to lasting peace. We call on all those present and those not present to reject apartheid and its past and present supporters. Your place and mine is in the democratic camp to which the Mahatma belonged. Attaining our liberation cannot be an easy and smooth task. We shall obtain it through our collective efforts. May the new Gandhi hall serve all the people of South Africa and may it serve the cause of Peace, Justice and Reconciliation.[12]

Consequently, Mandela considered nonviolence, whether social, political, or economic, as a battle of compassion, love, and fearlessness. But Mandela's compassionate fellowship had another side to it: a side more ethical than political, which aimed at a common humanity. He knew that nonviolence was the province of those who were undaunted and had moral courage. But, he also knew that such human beings needed to be truth-loving, empathetic, and self-transformative. Actually, Mandela is one of the rare leaders at the end of the twentieth century who was able to gain a moral capital through his empathetic ethics and with a self-conscious respect for the otherness of the Other. Though not a principled nonviolent leader with a very strong belief concerning *ahimsa* or *Agape* love, Mandela was a compassionate leader who did not separate between realistic politics and ethics of empathy. Mandela was fully cognizant of the fact that ethics of empathy was always accompanied by a change of heart and mind. In *Conversations with Myself*, he writes about his encounter with members of the Inuit community in Canada. He wrote:

In Canada, at a place called Goose Bay we stopped there to refill before we crossed over to Dublin, and as I was walking to the airport building I saw some people just outside the fence of the airport and I asked... the official who was taking us to the airport building "Now who are those?" He says "... those are Eskimos". Now I had never seen an Eskimo and I had always thought of them as people who are catching... polar bears and seals... I thought I should go and see these people.... And I was grateful that I did that because these were young people in their teens, late teens.... And as I chatted to them I was *amazed* to find out that these were high school children. They knew-they had heard that we were going to land and refill and... I was very happy to meet them and was tremendously impressed because they knew about the release, they watched the release and also they knew one or two meetings which I had addressed. And it was the *most* fascinating conversation precisely because it was *shocking*. I was *rudely* shocked, awakened to the fact that my knowledge of the Eskimo community was very backward because I never imagined that [they] were [at] schools... and [that] they were just like ourselves. I never imagined that. Although I was in the struggle, the freedom struggle I should have... know[n] that people *anywhere*, throughout the world, change from their less advanced positions.... I enjoyed that conversation very much... but the result... is that I caught.... pneumonia.[13]

Mandela was well-known for his love of children and young people, and that is why and how he got to meet members of Canada's Inuit community between two flights.

As such, Mandela's struggle for a compassionate fellowship around the world was, at the same time, a way for humanity to expand its capacity to rethink social life in terms of an ethics of empathy, a politics of forgiveness, and a revolution of values. But more than anything else, it was a struggle for a plural society in which all persons of all races, languages, and opinions can live together in harmony and with equal opportunity. Either as

Common Humanity and Ethics of Empathy 109

an activist, as a prisoner, or as a leader in government, Nelson Mandela remained intensely conscious of his moral and political responsibilities as a man in search for empathy and compassion. He developed the same idea at his acceptance speech at the Nobel Prize ceremony in December 1993. He underlined:

This reward will not be measured in money. Nor can it be reckoned in the collective price of the rare metals and precious stones that rest in the bowels of the African soil we tread in the footsteps of our ancestors. It will and must be measured by the happiness and welfare of the children, at once the most vulnerable citizens in any society and the greatest of our treasures... The value of our shared reward will and must be measured by the joyful peace which will triumph, because the common humanity that bonds both black and white into one human race, will have said to each one of us that we shall all live like the children of paradise... We do not believe that this Nobel Peace Prize is intended as a commendation for matters that have happened and passed. We hear the voices which say that it is an appeal from all those, throughout the universe, who sought an end to the system of apartheid. We understand their call, that we devote what remains of our lives to the use of our country's unique and painful experience to demonstrate, in practice, that the normal condition for human existence is democracy, justice, peace, non-racism, non-sexism, prosperity for everybody, a healthy environment and equality and solidarity among the peoples. Moved by that appeal and inspired by the eminence you have thrust upon us, we undertake that we too will do what we can to contribute to the renewal of our world so that none should, in future, be described as the wretched of the earth. Let it never be said by future generations that indifference, cynicism or selfishness made us fail to live up to the ideals of humanism which the Nobel Peace Prize encapsulates. Let the strivings of us all, prove Martin Luther King Jr to have been correct, when

110   *Comparative Approaches to Compassion*

he said that humanity can no longer be tragically bound to the starless midnight of racism and war. Let the efforts of us all, prove that he was not a mere dreamer when he spoke of the beauty of genuine brotherhood and peace being more precious than diamonds or silver or gold.[14]

However romantic this might sound, Nelson Mandela's experience of compassionate fellowship and empathetic nation-building in South Africa has proven that it is possible for people to live without hatred, revenge, and violence. Mandela's experiments with compassion, therefore, became a blueprint for our century and centuries to come. In his beautiful obituary for Nelson Mandela, Ebrahim Moosa pointed to the connection between compassion and sense of justice and desire for freedom "as traits he courageously cultivated." According to Moosa:

The abundance of these characteristics enabled him to rise above others at crucial moments in his career. One such occasion was an abrupt turn during a bruising television debate with Mr. F.W. de Klerk, the Afrikaner leader with whom he negotiated the political transition and with whom he also shared the Nobel Peace Prize. After lashing out at de Klerk's party, a contrite Mandela softened and told the country: "The exchanges between Mr. de Klerk and me should not obscure one important fact. I think we are a shining example to the entire world of people drawn from different racial groups who have a common loyalty, a common love, to their common country … ." Then Mandela turned to de Klerk and said to him, "Sir, you are one of those I rely upon. We are going to face the problem of this country together." Then reaching out for de Klerk's hand, Mandela said: "I am proud to hold your hand for us to go forward." In the playbook of any other politician, to make such a concession would count as a weakness, but

Common Humanity and Ethics of Empathy 111

Mandela turned competitive politics into a supreme nation building venture.[15]

Nearly a decade after his death, the ethical legacy of Mandela remains unparalleled. This is due in great part to his unique place in the long history of compassion and nonviolence. His moral leadership proved Gandhi's claim that

> in every great cause it is not the number of fighters that counts but it is the quality of which they are made that becomes the deciding factor. The greatest men of the world have always stood alone. Take the great prophets Zoroaster, Buddha, Jesus, Muhammad—they all stood alone like many others whom I can name. But they had living faith in themselves and their God, and believing as they did that God was on their side, they never felt lonely.[16]

Like Gandhi, Martin Luther King, Jr. and other nonviolent leaders of history, Mandela served as a moral compass for humanity, but unlike so many politicians and activists, he pointed the needle of that compass toward compassion. His recourse to nonviolence appeared as a relentless search for an ethic of dialogue in the most difficult situation of political confrontation between Whites and Blacks in South Africa. Detailing his ascent from an anti-apartheid activist and Robben Island-jailed terrorist, to an icon of nonviolent reconciliation and forgiveness, Nelson Mandela finished his autobiography, *Long Walk to Freedom*, with the following paragraph:

> I have walked that long road to freedom. I have tried not to falter; I have made missteps along the way. But I have discovered the secret that after climbing a great hill, one only finds that there are many more hills to climb. I have taken a moment here

to rest, to steal a view of the glorious vista that surrounds me, to look back on the distance I have come. But I can only rest for a moment, for with freedom come responsibilities, and I dare not linger, for my long walk is not ended.[17]

Mandela was well aware of the fact that he had stepped into the stream of an ancient tradition of prophets of nonviolence who each, like the Buddha, Jesus, St. Francis, Gandhi, Martin Luther King, Jr., and Khan Abdul Ghaffar Khan, devoted all their energies toward the establishment of a civilization of compassion. As it happens, they were able to draw the noblest in humankind, and that is what enabled humanity to overcome its moments of darkness.

Conclusion: Spiritualizing Compassion and Nonviolence

Fragility is an unbending necessity which binds our existence to mortality. Humans are fragile beings not because they die, but because they know that they will die. So, death exists for us in thought, before existing in the act of dying. Death is not generally chosen, but if it is the case, it is "not usually chosen as an end in itself, but for some other reason."[1] Indeed, death as a reality of life has the same seductive force as love. We fear it, but we are also intoxicated by it. However, there is no contradiction between love and death. One can easily die of love. Simone Weil was a philosopher who took a radical view of Christian love and died by and for love. For her the power of love was stronger than the force of death. Following Weil, one can say that while death is destiny, love is a choice. It is by choice that human beings love other living beings. This choice is not necessarily sexual; it is also in relation with the metaphysics of life. As Schopenhauer argued, love is the affirmation of the will to live. He asserted:

> The growing inclination of two lovers is really already the will to live of the new individual which they can and desire to produce; nay, even in the meeting of their longing glances its new life breaks out, and announces itself as a future individuality harmoniously and well composed. They feel the longing for an actual union and fusing together into a single being, in order to live on only as this; and this longing receives its fulfilment

114 *Comparative Approaches to Compassion*

in the child which is produced by them, as that in which the qualities, transmitted by them both, fused and united in one being, live on.[2]

The fundamental metaphysics of loving described by Schopenhauer remained basic to his thinking of life. Needless to add that Schopenhauer considered compassion as a typically human form of sympathy that unites us with all beings who want to live. In other words, human love and compassion are due to the fact that we exist. As Simone Weil puts it beautifully, "the word of love holds us in his arms from the beginning."[3] As such, where there is no love and compassion, there is no human bond and all social relations end up either in rage and hatred or in disbelief and uncertainty. On the contrary, according to Weil, "belief in the existence of other human beings as such is love."[4] Simone Weil advocated in her philosophy a radical regeneration of the validity of love. What she held was that "the only organ of contact with existence is love."[5] Thus, the simple fact of loving is self-transformative. Actually, Jesus of Nazareth was quite aware of this fact,

> when he said to his disciples: "Love one another", it was not attachment he was laying down as their rule. As it was a fact that there were bonds between them due to the thoughts, the life, and the habits they shared, he commanded them to transform these bonds into friendship, so that they should not be allowed to turn into impure attachment or hatred.[6]

Perhaps all human beings, by the very act of love, are destined to be fragile. However, the interesting point is that love stops the absolute violence of this fragility. But where there is room for love, there is room for compassion and justice. And as it happens, everything which originates from compassion points to beauty.

Conclusion 115

The truth of this beauty is in the act of caring for the otherness of the Other. But why do we have to care for the otherness of the Other? Because we want "humaneness." As Confucius asserts, "Is humaneness really so far away? If I desire humaneness, humaneness will surely come."[7] However, humaneness never comes into being with abstinence; it comes with effort and struggle. Humaneness is not a blank idea; it is a mode of action. Humaneness is always at the beginning. The end to achieve is to attain the otherness of the Other. As we say in Latin: *Finis Origine Pendet* (The end depends upon the beginning). However, humaneness is not only about following the Other. It is a response to the challenge of life. Here arises a responsibility which implies a revolution of values. Living wisely is the greatest revolution of values. The Self turns toward the Other, because it cannot remain enclosed and insensitive to the art of living. The Self cancels the tyrant within itself and turns toward the Other. The Self knows that it is condemned to live and die with the Other. It is interesting how the Self and the Other can create a community of hope against the fatality of hatred and indifference that could at any moment close in upon them. Yet, it is fallacious to think that religion is the only way for a community of hope to exist. Many benefactors of the human history were perfect agnostics. Let us listen to what Swami Vivekananda has to say about Gautama Buddha. He declares: "I would like to see moral men like Gautama Buddha who did not believe in a Personal God or a personal soul, never asked even about them but was a perfect agnostic, and yet was ready to lay down his life for anyone, and worked all his life for the good of all."[8] Therefore, if humaneness is left with any meaning in this world, it certainly means nothing but the recognition of the otherness of the Other, which cannot divorce itself from compassion. If nonviolent revolt against injustice is the right action of the mind, compassion is the adequate move of the heart. When the otherness of the Other bursts upon the Self, the Self becomes what we can call "compassion-intoxicated." Once the Self is compassionate toward the Other, compassion can change its mode of thinking the world. In other words, compassion is the recognition of the sacredness of the living being. Without compassion, interconnectedness becomes egoism and pride. This is what Lao Tzu calls "the virtue of non-contention." As the *Tao Te Ching* argues, "If you protect yourself with compassion you will be impervious."[9] The "virtue of non-contention" leads to the spirit of non-conquest. Conquest has always an aggressive quality: it dominates the Other, and hence creates an opposition to itself. Unlike what many people continue to think after 5,000 years of human history, conquest does not bring us anything that we do not yet have. It is, therefore, a meaningless action. On the contrary, compassion gains the trust, friendship, and partnership of the Other. There is a beautiful quote by Mandela which says: "If you want to make peace with your enemy, you have to work with your enemy. Then he becomes your partner."[10]

Human civilization needs to choose between the spirit of compassion and that of conquest. Let us not forget that the two predominant principles in the modern project of sovereignty and techno-science have been "*conquest*" and "*domination*." Descartes develops the idea of domination of Mother Earth by modern civilization with the promise of mastery and possession of Nature by modern science. On the other hand, the Spanish colonization of the Americas presents itself as the true expression of a double conquest: that of Nature by modern reason and that of Native Americans by the Conquistadors. Bartolomé de Las Casas and Francisco de Vitoria addressed the fundamental moral and

Conclusion 117

legal questions raised when Europe invaded America. Las Casas opposed the idea supported by Sepulveda and many other Spanish scholars of the time, arguing that the Indians were in fact such brutal beings that war against them was morally just. Assuredly, the great battle of compassion was fought by Las Casas against Sepulveda at Valladolid in 1550–1.

> We have no reason to be surprised at the defects, at the uncivilized and excessive customs which we may encounter among the Indian nations, nor to despise them for this. For most if not all the nations of the world have been even more perverted, irrational and depraved, and shown even less caution and wisdom in their manner of government and in their exercise of moral virtues. We ourselves have been much worse in the times of our ancestors and in the length and breadth of our span, as much by the excess and the confusion of manners as by our vices and bestial customs.[11]

These phrases, written by fray Bartolomé de Las Casas in his book *Apologetica Historia*, reflect that the Spanish discovery and subsequent conquest of the New World inspired a serious, if not heated, intellectual controversy regarding the necessity of compassion and humaneness in regard to the Indians. The controversy of Valladolid inaugurated a new debate on the concept of "compassionate civilization." Aristotle had already differentiated between human groups, namely the civilized and the barbarians. For Aristotle, the latter were naturally subservient to the former, because for them passion prevailed over reason. Sepúlveda applied this theory to the Indians. According to him, the Indians were a barbarian race whose natural, inferior condition entitled the Spaniards to wage war on them. On the contrary, Las Casas came to conclude that since the Indians were civilized human beings, Spaniards had no right to subject them either to slavery or to war. He suggested the ethics of compassion and empathetic dialogue toward the Indians. Therefore, the Las Casas-Sepúlveda controversy became a debate about compassion toward the otherness of the Other. This debate continues to be of a high significance for us in the twenty-first century. Its legacy lies in the idea of understanding and addressing the conditions of the "Other" from the Other's perspective.

Once, when asked what he thought of Western civilization, Mahatma Gandhi replied, "I think it would be a good idea."[12] By that he meant that humanity was still in the process of civilizing itself by taming its structural violence. In truth, civilization is a potentiality which owes its realization to the coexistence and cooperation of all cultures and traditions of thought. But human civilization is a journey, not a destination. Therefore, it is an unfinished project. We are deluding ourselves if we claim that we have arrived at an achieved civilization. The struggle for a civilization of compassion and nonviolence continues, because this is where humankind can find its greatness. As Teilhard de Chardin affirmed: "We must strive for ever more greatness; but we cannot do so if we are faced by the prospect of an eventual decline, a disaster at the end."[13] Whether we like it or not, the greatness Teilhard is referring to is essentially moral and based on an attitude of indebtedness to the Other. Truly speaking, the whole philosophy of nonviolence is based on the awareness of the Self that it is indebted to the Other. Martin Luther King explained this element of being indebted to the Other in the following terms:

> We are everlasting debtors to known and unknown men and women. When we arise in the morning, we go into the bathroom where we reach for a sponge which is provided for

Conclusion 119

us by a Pacific Islander. We reach for soap that is created for us by a European. Then at the table we drink coffee which is provided for us by a South American, or tea by a Chinese or cocoa by a West African. Before we leave for our jobs we are already beholden to more than half the world.[14]

In the same manner of thinking, Simone Weil used the concept of "loan" as something of value which needs to be renewed. She wrote: "Everything without exception which is of value in me comes from somewhere other than myself, not as a gift but as a loan which must be ceaselessly renewed. Everything without exception which is in me is absolutely valueless; and, among the gifts which have come to me from elsewhere, everything which I appropriate becomes valueless immediately I do so."[15] The characteristic of a loan is its reciprocity. A loan is something which is given by the Self to the Other, but at the same time it needs to be renewed by the Other. In the same spirit, compassion is a human virtue which needs to be renewed with humans and with the world. As such, humanity will continue to exist, only and only if human beings continue to have compassion for each other. In the same way, the world will continue to exist only if there is love of the world (*Amor Mundi*). Therefore, one of the indispensable movements of the human soul is to inject love into the world, but also to dilute its own miseries in the love that is given back by the world. This mature relationship between the humankind and the world is only possible if humanity achieves spiritual growth. Unless we feel that there is such a thing as a spiritual growth of humankind, the compassionate civilization will not be fulfilled. That is why, to be truly spiritual is to serve humankind. Such a view of spirituality as compassion and nonviolence will bring peoples nearer to one another and forget their partisan strife. We can tie here the concept of compassion to the idea of peaceful

120 Comparative Approaches to Compassion

coexistence which is identical with the world's multiplicity and plurality. The important thing is that humanity has the potential to overcome violence and hatred and adopt compassionate fellowship. As Sarvepalli Radhakrishnan mentions:

> Let us remember that in this world there have been many civilizations, one after the other—Babylon, Argyria, Greek. When you look into the history of those civilizations, you will discover one fundamental fact; those which laid the stress on matter, on weapons, on arms, have passed away, those which laid their stress on the development of friendship, love, brotherhood, have survived.[16]

Conscious of the fact that cultural, religious, and national distances need to be bridged, this struggle for a compassionate fellowship cannot exist without the ideal of universal synthesis between the East and the West. At this point, we should turn to the great spiritual poet of India, Rabindranath Tagore, who in his devotion to compassion, harmony, and peace, denounced fanaticism, nationalism, hatred, and violence.

Tagore had no magic formula for arriving at a compassionate fellowship between the East and the West. He saw the future of compassionate fellowship in the idea of a universal humanism represented by global solidarity of all human beings irrespective of religion, nationality, or culture. Thus, there were no place for hatred, exclusion, and violence in Tagore's idea of universal civilization. For Tagore, a compassionate civilization was where human beings of different cultures would be united together and in unison with the world. The idea of universalism of Rabindranath Tagore was that of a larger humanity hold together by inescapable moral links beyond the boundaries created by racialism, nationalism, and all other forms of segregation and fanaticism. He wrote: "We are today to build

Conclusion 121

the future of man on an honest understanding of our varied racial personality which gives richness to life, on tolerance and sympathy and cooperation in the great task of liberating the human mind from the dark forces of unreason and mutual distrust of homicidal pride of sect and lust of gain."[17] Tagore considered nationalism and sectarian violence as important obstacles to the recognition of the otherness of the Other and a compassionate companionship between individuals and among nations. In a letter to Leonard Elmhirst in 1939, he affirmed: "It does not need a defeatist to feel deeply anxious about the future of millions who... are being simultaneously subjected... the seething discontents of communalism."[18] He believed that the best way to create a civilization of solidarity, sympathy, and dialogue was to educate citizens to be interested in their own cultural heritage, while learning about the manners of action and thought of others. Isaiah Berlin saw in this Tagorian attitude a duality that he expressed in the following terms:

> "Tagore stood fast on the narrow causeway, and did not betray his vision of the difficult truth. He condemned romantic over-attachment to the past, what he called the tying of India to the past 'like a sacrificial goat tethered to a post,' and he accused men who displayed it—they seemed to him reactionary—of not knowing what true political freedom was, pointing out that it is from English thinkers and English books that the very notion of political liberty was derived. But against cosmopolitanism he maintained that the English stood on their own feet, and so must Indians. In 1917 he once more denounced the danger of 'leaving everything to the unalterable will of the Master,' be he Brahmin or Englishman."[19]

Tagore was strongly against religious fanaticism and nationalist separatism, which created divisions among human beings.

Consequently, Tagore's philosophy of compassionate fellowship and global solidarity took much care for interdependence of nations and interconnectedness of individuals in terms of dialogue of cultures. The Tagorian idea of a dialogical civilization was aimed at educating a compassionate humanity able to transcend social and cultural stereotypes and mental ghettos. Tagore's adherence to the concept of otherness of the Other reveals a constant emphasis on the idea of "unitive empathy." He not only attempted to revive the concept of compassionate companionship, but also tried to re-interpret it in the mirror of humanitarian values. Yet, Tagore never had an idealized view of the past. His idea of return to India's civilizational values was not nostalgic. His analysis of a compassionate civilization was an open and inclusive project of empathetic harmony among individuals and culture. As he affirmed, "Civilization must be judged and prized, not by the amount of power it has developed, but by how much it has evolved and given expression to, by its laws and institutions, the love of humanity."[20] As such, Tagore's idea of a universal compassion at the level of human civilization resulted from the contrast that he established between the egoistic and utilitarian attitude of living in the world and the effort to foster responsibility and empathy in the universe. In other words, he believed that humanity's worth was in the nature of its civilizational process. "Whenever some ancient civilization fell into decay and died," Tagore asserted,

> it was owing to causes which produced callousness of heart and led to the cheapening of man's worth; when either the state or some powerful group of men began to look upon the people as a mere instrument of their power; when, by compelling weaker races to slavery and trying to keep them down by every means, man struck at the foundation of his greatness, his own love of

Conclusion 123

freedom and fair-play. Civilisation can never sustain itself upon cannibalism of any form. For that by which alone man is true can only be nourished by love and justice.[21]

By extending his vision of civilization beyond the bounds of mere particularism, Tagore placed the idea of an empathetic world as a supreme value. For him, the empathetic world should be viewed as a single family, where different nations were its members, each contributing its quota to the welfare of the whole. Tagore was persuaded that this empathetic civilization, as an intercultural whole, had to renew all communities and all individuals. Civilization, therefore, made sense for him only if it directly confronted the ecology of violence and the moral incapacity to love. That is why, he wrote: "Our will has freedom in order that it may find out that its true course is towards goodness and love. For goodness and love are infinite, and only in the infinite is the perfect realization of freedom possible."[22] Consequently, Tagore insisted on the idea of love as the expression of the oneness of our soul with the world. For him, love was not a result of compulsion, but that of joy. From his point of view, the world was born of love and sustained by it. Thus, Tagore considered human fellowship in relation to the compassionate love of Nature and humanity. He believed that humanity was in perpetual search of the everlasting joy and rhythm of nonviolence in the stream of Nature. He wrote: "We realize that Peace is true and not conflict, Love is true and not hatred; and Truth is the One, not the disjointed multitude."[23] Interestingly, Tagore considered the aesthetic experience of Nature as a joy of compassionate companionship, which consisted of being lifted out of oneself and being identified with the otherness of Nature. As such, for him, the aesthetic experience of the world was not only an outwardization of the self toward the world, but

124   *Comparative Approaches to Compassion*

equally an inwardization of the world toward the self. "This world which takes its form in the mould of Man's perception," affirms Tagore in his book *Personality*, "still remains as partial world of his senses and mind. It is like a guest and not like a kinsman. It becomes completely our own when it comes within the range of our emotions. With our love and hatred, pleasure and pain, fear and wonder continually working upon it, this world becomes a part of our personality."[24] Actually, Tagore used the two concepts of beauty and truth each time that he talks about a loving relation and compassionate companionship with the world. That is why, in the manner of Keats, he wrote: "Beauty is truth's smile when she beholds her own face in a perfect mirror."[25] Tagore saw the compassionate companionship of humankind with the world in the great nonviolent union with Nature. He, therefore, revolted against the modern uncompassionate mastery of Nature and affirmed:

When we look at the world through the veil of our desires we make it small and narrow, and fail to perceive its full truth. Of course it is obvious that the world serves us and fulfils our needs, but our relation to it does not end there. We are bound to it with a deeper and truer bond than that of necessity. Our soul is drawn to it; our love of life is really our wish to continue our relation with this great world. This relation is one of love. We are glad that we are in it; we are attached to it with numberless threads, which extend from this earth to the stars. Man foolishly tries to prove his superiority by imagining his radical separateness from what he calls his physical world, which, in his blind fanaticism, he sometimes goes to the extent of ignoring altogether, holding it at his direst enemy. Yet the more his knowledge progresses, the more it becomes difficult for man to establish this separateness, and all the imaginary boundaries he

Conclusion   125

had set up around himself vanish one after another. Every time we lose some of our badges of absolute distinction by which we conferred upon our humanity the right to hold itself apart from its surroundings, it gives us a shock of humiliation. But we have to submit to this. If we set up our pride on the path of our self-realisation to create divisions and disunion, then it must sooner or later come under the wheels of truth and be ground to dust. No, we are not burdened with some monstrous superiority, unmeaning in its singular abruptness. It would be utterly degrading for us to live in a world immeasurably less than ourselves in the quality of soul, just as it would be repulsive and degrading to be surrounded and served by a host of slaves, day and night, from birth to the moment of death. On the contrary, this world is our compeer, nay, we are one with it.[26]

As we can see, in the line of thought of thinkers like Gandhi, Aurobindo, Merton, Thoreau etc., Tagore considered Nature primarily as a reservoir of peace and nonviolence to which humanity could refer for regeneration. According to Tagore, since God is present in Nature, we ought to love Nature to fulfill and realize ourselves. Thus, Tagore saw love for God as a compassionate fellowship for Nature and humankind. This pantheistic worldview in Tagore resulted from the formative influences of the *Upanishads* and the *Bhagavad Gita* on him. He inherited the Upanishadic idea of a living presence of God in all created objects and the presence of "self-luminous Brahman" in the hearts of all human beings. For Tagore, there was a sense of interconnectedness between the physical and the spiritual, and between the ontological and the ethical. He considered life as a continuous process of synthesis between the ideal and the real. Maybe that is why, he was unshakably convinced of human unity and solidarity. Coincidentally, Tagore believed that human's love

126   *Comparative Approaches to Compassion*

for humanity was a great expression of the fulfillment of the compassionate fellowship. He wrote:

> It is significant that all great religions have their historic origin in persons who represented in their life a truth which was not cosmic and unmoral, but human and good. They rescued religion from the magic stronghold of demon force and brought it into the inner heart of humanity, into the fulfilment not confined to some exclusive good fortune of the individual but to the welfare of all men. This was not for the spiritual ecstasy of lonely souls, but for the spiritual emancipation of all races. They came as the messengers of Man to men of all countries and spoke of the salvation that could only be reached by the perfecting of our relationship with Man the Eternal, Man the Divine. Whatever might be their doctrines of God, or some dogmas that they borrowed from their own time and tradition, their life and teaching had the deeper implication of a being who is the infinite in man, the Father, the Friend, the Lover, whose service must be through serving all mankind. For the God in man depends upon men's service and men's love for his own love's fulfilment.[27]

With the idea of compassionate fellowship in mind, Tagore rejected all forms of regimentation and standardization of human beings. He, therefore, founded his theory of education on an empathetic sense of interconnectedness between human beings and the surrounding world. Tagore believed that education must develop the personality of humans in the context of Nature and allow individuals to be in tune with the logic of the world. Through his various educational experiences at Santineketan, Tagore arrived at the conclusion that education is deeply rooted in Nature. As a matter of fact, he emphasized on a unison between education and life. For this reason, he suggested that education should revolve

Conclusion 127

compassionately and empathetically around Nature, accompanied with classes held in the open-air and excursions organized in natural surroundings. According to Tagore, the education of compassion and generosity, as well as that of awareness and responsibility in regard to the world united all races, cultures, and nations with the vision of oneness of humankind. This underlying belief explained the seriousness of Tagore toward a genuine sense of world unity and compassionate companionship among human beings. He believed that a dialogue among religions could provide such a compassionate and empathetic comradeship. According to him, "It is high time for us to know how much more important it is, in the present age, to be able to understand the fundamental truth of all religions and realise their essential unity, thus clearing the way for a world-wide spiritual comradeship, than to preach some special religion of our own with all its historical limitations."[28] Tagore believed that humankind should realize a unity, "wider in rage, deeper in sentiment, stronger in power than ever before."[29] But Tagore was well aware of the fact that, in order to be realized, this unity needed a new vision of humankind. This vision unfolded the dynamic character of life in relation with Truth, Beauty, and Compassion. As such, Tagore's belief in a world with multiple voices which enabled moral and aesthetic fusions between East and West, encouraged an overriding commitment to universal compassionate fellowship. Until the end of his life, Rabindranath Tagore continued to have faith in what he called "the spirit of Man." In his last essay, written in April 1941, he wrote, "As I look around I see the crumbling ruins of a proud civilization strewn like a vast heap of futility. And yet I shall not commit the grievous sin of losing faith in Man."[30] Tagore knew well that the Self could not find its truth in its separateness from the Other, but in the spirit of unity. He also knew that the stream of unity runs through compassion and love. As he affirmed: "In love, all the contradictions of existence merge themselves and are lost. Only in love are unity and duality not at variance. Love must be one and two at the same time."[31] An Indian contemporary of Tagore, Sri Aurobindo, also had a deep vision of the spiritual unity of humankind. His philosophy of human evolution and integral yoga was a reminder of the long journey of the idea of compassion from the oriental religions like Buddhism, Jainism, and Hinduism to the great thinkers of nonviolence in the twentieth century.

As an Indian nationalist, social philosopher, and yogi, Sri Aurobindo was interested in both spiritual matters and secular issues. He was particularly a yogi engaged in *dharma yuddha* (fighting for the supremacy of right over might). His mature ideas found their touchstone in the idea of human unity, but he truly believed all his life that such a spiritual unity would not be possible unless it is preceded by a general change in humankind's consciousness. Nevertheless, he made it clear in the last chapter of his book *The Life Divine* that the spiritual transformation of humanity had nothing to do with religion.

There is the possibility in the swing back from a mechanistic idea of life and society the human mind may seek refuge in a return to the religious idea and a society governed or sanctioned by religion. But organized religion, though it can provide a means of inner uplift for the individual and preserve in it or behind it a way for his opening to spiritual experience, has not changed human life and society; it could not do so because, in governing society, it had to compromise with the lower parts of life and could not insist on the inner change of the whole being; it could insist only on a creedal adherence, a formal acceptance of its

Conclusion 129

ethical standards and a conformity to institution, ceremony and ritual... A total spiritual direction given to the whole life and the whole nature can alone lift humanity beyond itself.[32]

Aurobindo summed up the nature of Man in the ideal of a united human society. This unity, according to Sri Aurobindo, could not take place unless Man's vital and mental nature was uplifted by a spiritual Supernature. Therefore, if true human unity is to be achieved Man needs "to pursue its upward evolution towards the finding of expression of the Divine... taking full advantage of the free development and gains of all individuals and nations and groupings of men, to work towards the day when mankind may be really and not ideally one family."[33] In other words, the Divine descends into Cosmic being, while Man ascends through the medium of a Supermind toward the Divine. Therefore, there is a double movement at work here. Man is eternally seeking the ultimate Reality, which Aurobindo called *Saccidananda* using the Vedantic vocabulary. "Saccidananda," asserted Sri Aurobindo, "is the unknown." Reality is *sat, cit,* and *ananda,* which Aurobindo translated by the three concepts of pure existence, conscious force, and the delight of existence. The goal is "the out flowering of the Divine in collective humanity."[34] The ideal, said Aurobindo, is the free unity of mankind. "Today," wrote Aurobindo in his book *The Ideal of Human Unity,* "the ideal of human unity is more or less vaguely making its way to the forefront of our consciousness... (It) is evidently a part of Nature's eventual scheme and must come about."[35]

For Aurobindo, the evolutionary process of compassionate fellowship of humanity was possible not through rationality, but through Yogic experience. The way which leads to the divine life is

130   *Comparative Approaches to Compassion*

"integral yoga." This is why Aurobindo believed that every human being is a Yogi, but not a conscious one. Those who have become conscious of this process through the Yogic experience can help the others. The simple reason to this is that "All mankind is one in nature... Nothing which any individual race or nation can triumphantly realize... has any permanent value except in so far as it adds something for this human march."[36] In other words, Sri Aurobindo was against the old idea of separation of politics from religion and, therefore, to him nationalism was a spiritual process. "Nationalism is not a mere political program," wrote Aurobindo in his daily paper entitled *Bande Mataram,*

> nationalism is a religion that has come from God; nationalism is a creed which you shall have to live.... If you are going to be a nationalist, if you are going to assent to this religion of nationalism, you must do it in the religious spirit. You must remember that you are the instruments of God... Then there will be a blessing on our work and this great nation will rise again and become once more what it was in the days of spiritual greatness. You are the instruments of God to save the light, to save the spirit of India from lasting obscuration and abasement.[37]

We can see clearly how compassion and empathy play as social and political concepts in shaping the idea of human unity in Aurobindo's mind. Aurobindo based his demand for independence on the Romantic idea of the nation-soul. In his early writings, he talked about the "soul of India" and in his speeches and writings in 1907–8, he defined nationalism as a civic religion. In another speech, he went further and equated Indian nationalism with the *sanatana dharma*. Yet, Aurobindo was not interested in perpetuating Hinduism as a sectarian religion. What

Conclusion   131

he was interested in was "a new synthesis of religious thought and experience, a new religious world-life from intolerance, yet full of faith and fervor, accepting all forms of religion because it has an unshakable faith in the One."[38] However, for Aurobindo this new synthesis had to go hand in hand with the inalienable right of nations to independence, simply because being ruled by foreigners was an unjust and unnatural condition. "Political freedom," Aurobindo declared in 1907, "is the life breath of a nation: to attempt social reform, educational reform, industrial expansion, the moral improvement of race, without aiming first and foremost at political freedom is the very height of ignorance and futility."[39] In fact, from his early writings Aurobindo was keen to see India play a leading role in the world. This was because he saw the great stage of human progress as a moral and spiritual one and he believed that India had a lot to teach Europe. As a matter of fact, Aurobindo considered Europe as parceled out in nations, but in his view India was an old civilization. India, according to Aurobindo, had a special place in Asia. Thus, Asia from his point of view, was

> the custodian of world's peace of mind, the physician of the maladies which Europe generates. She is commissioned to rise from time to time from her ages of self-communion, self-sufficiency, self-absorption and rule the world for a season... when the restless spirit of Europe has added a new phase of discovery to the evolution of the science of material life, has regulated politics, re-based society, remodeled law, rediscovered science, the spirit of Asia, calm, contemplative, self-possessed, takes possession of Europe's discovery and corrects its exaggeration, its aberrations by intuition, the spiritual light she alone can turn the world. Asia has always initiated, Europe completed. The strength of Europe is in details, the strength

of Asia is in synthesis… It is therefore the office of Asia to take up the work of human evolution, when Europe comes to a standstill and loses itself in a clash of vain speculations, barren experiments and helpless struggles to escape from the consequences of her own mistakes. Such a time has now come in world's history.[40]

In the manner of Gandhi and Tagore, Sri Aurobindo was a true believer in a dialogue of cultures. Therefore, he was not in favor of an isolated India, but he was also against a blind imitation of the West. As a matter of fact, according to him, India's imitation of the Western society was not only a mistake for India, but also for the whole world. "If India follows in the footsteps of Europe," wrote Aurobindo, "accepts her political ideals, social system, economic principles, she will be overcome with the same maladies."[41] Aurobindo was convinced that if India wants to survive as an independent state it had to be conscious about its spiritual force and its diversity. Indian unity would be achieved because of Indian diversity. "Diversity," proclaimed Sri Aurobindo, "is as necessary as unity to our true completeness."[42] However, Aurobindo considered unity and uniformity as the law of life. Even though Aurobindo felt the world union as the ultimate goal, he saw the nation as a "necessary unit" and an "indestructible" force. For him there was a limit to nationalism in general. According to Aurobindo, the progress of the civilization depended on its advance toward human unity. "The perfect society," affirmed Aurobindo, "will be that which most entirely favors the perfection of the individual; the perfection of the individual will be incomplete if it does not help him towards the perfect state of the social aggregate to which he belongs and eventually

Conclusion 133

to that of the largest possible human aggregate, the whole of a united humanity."[43]

Aurobindo saw the perfection of the individual as a widening and a heightening in human and cosmic development. This heightening results in the integration of all levels of life and the achievement of unicity by the mind. As such salvation for Aurobindo does not have a religious meaning. It is a rebirth of Man as a supramental being. "Man," writes Aurobindo,

> is a transitional being; he is not final. For in man and high beyond him ascend the radiant degrees that climb to a divine supermanhood. There lies our destiny and the liberating key to our aspiring but troubled and limited mundane existence... Supermind is superman; a Gnostic supermanhood is the next distinct and triumphant evolutionary step to be reached by earthly nature.[44]

In other words, the Supermind helps Man to achieve integral realization of his personality and of ultimate reality. The Supermind is, according to Aurobindo, the supreme truth-consciousness. It is the infinite principle of knowledge. It is the necessary link between the existence, consciousness, and bliss (*Sachchidananda*) and the phenomenal worlds of life and mind. As long as the mind is separated from the Supermind it perceives only the particular and not the universal. That is to say, "the mind cannot possess the infinite... it can only lie blissfully helpless under the luminous shadow of the Real cast down on it from planes of existence beyond its reach."[45] The Supermind, therefore, can bring a big spiritual change in the nature of Man making possible the new integral personality. Agreeing that realization of non-duality is the purpose of life, Sri Aurobindo holds that each unique individual has a singular path to realization of integral non-dualism. For this reason, he insists that daily action is itself the means of realization. Just as one practices yoga for the purpose of developing one's inner spirituality, so participation in worldly experience is of the same importance. This is true because, as Aurobindo insists, "All life is yoga." In other words, the integral yoga prepares the conditions for the descent of Supermind. The yogi realizes himself through the cosmos and through the social life. This is why Aurobindo believes that the process of evolution has a purpose, which is advancing ineluctably toward the realization of the Life Divine here on Earth.

Sri Aurobindo elaborated his educational ideas in relation with his ideals of nonviolence, human unity, and "travel towards divine perfection."[46] For him, the goal of education was the study of the human mind, because he considered the mind as the principal instrument of knowledge. Thus the aim of education, according to Aurobindo was: "the building of the powers of the human mind and spirit – the evoking of knowledge and will and the power to use knowledge, character, culture."[47] For Aurobindo, Man had to be transformed and spiritualized through the educational practice. This process began with self-knowledge which is self-mastery and it brings ultimately the transformation of Man into a spiritual being.

Let us not forget that, Aurobindo was also a key spiritual figure in the twentieth century who suggested the idea of spiritualization of compassion. For him, the major task was to awaken the aspiration for the divine in the body and in the mind of human beings. Thus, Aurobindo put the weight of education on the supramental and the discovery of the psychic being. In his book *The Human Cycle*, he affirmed:

> The true secret whether with child, or man, is to help him find his deeper self, the real psychic entity within. That, if we ever

Conclusion 135

give it a chance to come forward, and still more, if we call it into the foreground as "the leader of the march set in our front", will itself take up most of the business of education out of our hands and develop the capacity of the psychological being towards a realization of potentialities.[48]

Likewise, Aurobindo's integral yoga contended that the union with the Divine Supermind was possible through a complete cooperation with the cosmic creative power. "Yoga," asserted Aurobindo, "is the exchange of an egoistic for a universal or cosmic consciousness lifted towards or informed by the super-cosmic, transcendent Unnamable who is the source and support of all things."[49] Yoga and education are one and the same process through which spirituality emerges in mind. That is why the eternal truths of ancient wisdom had an appeal to Sri Aurobindo. According to him, spirituality unlike religion does not lay excessive stress on dogmas. "A total spiritual direction given to the whole life and whole nature can alone lift humanity beyond itself,"[50] wrote Aurobindo in his book *The Life Divine*. For it is true that, according to Aurobindo, without the higher spirit, the lower mind cannot be spiritualized.

As a spiritual internationalist who believed in the compassionate fellowship of humankind, Aurobindo put a lot of emphasis on the transcendent aspect of Man. For him the only answer to the crisis in the human world was an enlightened awareness of the spiritual unity of our existence through which a sustainable compassionate fellowship could be achieved. "The truth of the Spirit," wrote Aurobindo, "may step in and lead humanity to the path of its highest possible happiness and perfection."[51] However, for Sri Aurobindo, the perfection was yet to come, because the goal of spiritualization of compassion was the creation of spiritual human beings and spiritual

136 *Comparative Approaches to Compassion*

communities. As such, Aurobindo's goal was mainly aimed at achieving a spiritualized and compassionate community. This spiritualized community based on compassionate fellowship would not have nation-states fighting with each other, because in such a community men are not egoistic and look beyond their self-interests. Similarly, Aurobindo defined human unity as "the attempt of human mind and life to grow out of national idea and form and even in a way to destroy it, in the interest of larger synthesis of mankind."[52] Because of this, Aurobindo saw a common destiny and a common hope for both the East and the West. "East and West," he wrote in 1949,

> have the same human nature, a common human destiny, the same aspiration after a greater perfection, the same seeking after something higher than itself, something towards which inwardly and outwardly we move.... East and West could be reconciled in the pursuit of the highest and largest ideal, Spirit embrace Matter and Matter find its own true reality and the hidden Reality in all things in the Spirit.[53]

Many rightly consider Sri Aurobindo next to Gandhi, Tagore, and Abdul Ghaffar Khan as one of the great architects of nonviolence in modern India. But the foundations laid by these men were for the edifice of universal compassionate fellowship and human unity which surpassed the national freedom movement in India. For all of them, universal compassionate fellowship was a message of diversity and not uniformity. "Uniformity," proclaimed Sri Aurobindo in an article in 1917, "is not the law of life. Life exists by diversity; it insists that every group, every being shall be, even while one with all the rest in its universality, yet by some principle or ordered detail of variation unique."[54] In other words,

Conclusion 137

spiritualization of compassion was a way to have a harmonious exchange with the otherness of the Other.

Witnessing the triumph of compassion over indifference, Gandhi was aware of the fact that the process of spiritualization of compassion appealed to the moral ability of each citizen to empathize with the experience of the Other. That is why he observed in 1939, that "*Swaraj* of a people means the sum total of the *swaraj* (self-rule) of individuals."[55] As we can see, spiritualized compassion, represented by the two dimensions of empathy and love, was integral to the whole Gandhian project of political emancipation. Hence, for Gandhi, emancipation and self-governance required a spiritual access and understanding of compassionate fellowship. Accordingly, Gandhi's initial efforts were directed toward the understanding and exercise of compassion for social and political transformation. Gandhi's genius was to spiritualize compassion by politicizing spirituality. Although a conscience-keeper of Indian civilization like Aurobindo and Tagore, Gandhi was also a spiritual unifier, who knew how to bring together the whole tradition of compassion from the teachings of the Buddha and the *Bhagavad Gita* to the *Sermon on the Mount* of Jesus Christ and Tolstoy's Christian mysticism. As such, Gandhi was a compassionate gadfly who believed in the power of nonviolence in shaping a compassionate humanity. If anything, nonviolence represents the spiritualization of compassion in action. As Gandhi explained: "It is not possible to make a person or a society nonviolent by compulsion." And he added:

> For me nonviolence is not a mere philosophical principle. It is the rule and the breath of my life. I now I fail often, sometimes

consciously, more often unconsciously. It is a matter not of the intellect but of the heart. True guidance comes by the constant waiting upon God, by utmost humility, self-abnegation, by being ever ready to sacrifice one's self. Its practice requires fearlessness and courage of the highest order.[56]

Setting the record straight, we can say that Gandhi's nonviolence continues to be a compassionately creative attitude for our world. In a deeper sense, it is a serious and conscientious commitment to a compassionate humanity, which struggles non-stop for what Martin Luther King, Jr. called a "Beloved Community." Both Gandhi and Martin Luther King, Jr. knew that nonviolent action was a social gesture that transcended ordinary trust or love. Accordingly, Gandhi wrote:

Mutual trust and mutual love are no trust and no love. The real love is to love them that hate you, to love your neighbour even though you distrust him. I have sound reasons for distrusting the English official world. If my love is sincere, I must love the Englishman in spite of my distrust. Of what avail is my love, if it be only so long as I trust my friend? Even thieves do that. They become enemies immediately the trust is gone.[57]

And Martin Luther King, Jr. added his own vision of love and trust by saying:

This call for a world-wide fellowship that lifts neighborly concern beyond one's tribe, race, class and nation is in reality a call for an all-embracing and unconditional love for all men. This oft misunderstood and misinterpreted concept— so readily dismissed by the Nietzsches of the world as a weak and cowardly force—has now become an absolute necessity for the survival of man. When I speak of love I am not speaking of some sentimental and weak response. I am speaking of that

Conclusion 139

force which all of the great religions have seen as the supreme unifying principle of life. Love is somehow the key that unlocks the door which leads to ultimate reality. This Hindu-Moslem-Christian-Jewish-Buddhist belief about ultimate reality is beautifully summed up in the first epistle of Saint John: "Let us love one another; for love is God and everyone that loveth is born of God and knoweth God. He that loveth not knoweth not God; for God is love. If we love one another God dwelleth in us, and his love is perfected in us."[58]

By reading these two quotes from Mahatma Gandhi and Martin Luther King, Jr. we can understand clearly and distinctly why and how the history of compassion joins hands with that of nonviolence. Both Mahatma Gandhi and Dr. King were familiar with the fact that nonviolence demanded the great exercise of compassion. But they also knew well that both compassion and nonviolence might fail as altruistic actions toward the otherness of the Other. In answer to the question "Is Nonviolence Ineffective," Gandhi wrote in 1939:

Every action is a resultant of a multitude of forces even of a contrary nature. There is no waste of energy. So we learn in the books on mechanics. This is equally true of human actions. The difference is that in the one case we generally know the forces at work, and when we do, we can mathematically foretell the resultant. In the case of human actions, they result from a concurrence of forces of most of which we have no knowledge. But our ignorance must not be made to serve the cause of disbelief in the power of these forces. Rather is our ignorance a cause for greater faith. And nonviolence being the mightiest force in the world and also the most elusive in its working, it demands the greatest exercise of faith. Even as we believe in God in faith, so have we to believe in nonviolence in faith.[59]

The lesson to be learnt from the history of nonviolence is that it plays a crucial role in responding to the shortcomings of compassionate politics and exclusive economic life in our world. The legacy of nonviolence lives on through the urgency of the presence of compassion in our daily lives. Also, the coronavirus pandemic has endangered our basic values and liberties and taught humanity that it is time to be more compassionate. Therefore, the spirit of the times takes us back to the canonic teachings of human history on compassion and nonviolence. This is the unique window of opportunity for humanity to save itself from its own evils. If humanity continues to remain heartless and indifferent toward the sufferings and miseries of its members, it will be on the road to its self-destruction. However, nonviolence is not a self-defeating method of struggle and that is why it seems to be compassionate. Truly, as Martin Luther King, Jr. formulated brilliantly, "Nonviolence is based on the conviction that the universe is on the side of justice. It is this deep faith in the future that causes the nonviolent resister to accept suffering without retaliation. He knows that in his struggle for justice he has cosmic companionship."[60] The genius of the prophets of compassion, like the Buddha, Mahavira, Jesus of Nazareth, St. Francis, Gandhi, Abdul Ghaffar Khan, Dr. King, Mandela, and many others, was their ability to perceive that humanity was able of compassion, a force which could transform the world.

This book ends where we started: the observation that human being is an ontologically fragile animal, capable of violence and compassion in a single lifetime. And yet, there are many moments in human history, where and when humanity has been unable to emphasize its fragility in order to save its noble presence in history. And if nonviolent humanism proved itself unable to

Conclusion 141

confront the power of evil in history, the two have seemed, in fact, to be bedfellows. How is it, then, that a small and fragile man from India, living in the first half of the twentieth century succeeded in resurrecting the messages of the Buddha and Jesus Christ, the day he decided to go on speaking and acting against social and political violence? Mahatma Gandhi knew well that his compassionate nonviolence could lead him to death. But, he also knew that death is the biological expression of *homo fragilis*. As Shakespeare says in his *Sonnets*: "So shalt thou feed on Death, that feeds on men."[61] However, what was important for Gandhi was not death, but change. We all die, however, we can change. Gandhi said: "We must become the change we want to see in the world." This quote reminds us of the fact that our destructive attitudes have been the basis of all problems and challenges in the history of mankind. Compassion and nonviolence are what we must cultivate in ourselves. Undoubtedly, humanity will be incapable of creating a framework for global peace without transcending its frailty and fragility and exercising a life of compassion. If there is an emancipative philosophy of Man's spiritual quest in history, it can be summarized in the message of compassion and nonviolence as foundations of a common humanity. What is so mysterious about *homo fragilis* is its tendency toward empathy, but also a moral attitude and inclination to comprehend and to share the suffering of other living beings. As such, *homo fragilis* is a being full of contradictions: it harms and hurts others by its violence, but it sympathizes and shows mercy and compassion toward the suffering of other living creatures. We are unhappy when others are unhappy, as we can learn to share the happiness of others. But learning does not come without listening and if humankind continues to approach its existence and the outside world without listening to one's inner voice and to the others, future generations will face stupendous challenges and difficulties. If there is only one message in all the philosophical and spiritual efforts of humankind, it is the moment of common humanity which takes a universal distance from the feelings of hate, selfishness, and intolerance. That is to say, compassion is an attitude of mind and heart that helps *homo fragilis* to cultivate the otherness of the Other in oneself. There is nothing original about an individual who celebrates compassion and nonviolence, but when it comes to human civilization, the wheels of Fate turn in another direction. No doubt, a civilization which is incapable of recognizing compassion and understanding nonviolence is a doomed civilization. Therefore, if the forces of love and compassion do not succeed, despite all bars and barriers, to win back the spiritual heritage of humanity, the spirit of violence which lies unvanquished in the psychology of *homo fragilis* shall shatter humankind's nobility of spirit and its creative urge to create the good and the beautiful.

Notes

Introduction

1   Kierkegaard, Soren, "Works of Love," in *The Essential Kierkegaard*, Princeton University Press, Princeton, 1997, p.311.

2   Merton, Thomas, *Love and Living*, A Harvest/HBJ Book, New York, 1985, p.27.

3   Kierkegaard, Soren, "Works of Love," pp.307–8.

4   Kundera, Milan, *The Unbearable Lightness of Being*, Harper & Row, New York, 1984, p.31.

5   Marcuse, Herbert, *Eros and Civilization*, Beacon Press, Boston, 1966, pp.xvii–xviii.

6   Merton, Thomas, *Love and Living*, p.34.

7   Fromm, Erich, *The Art of Loving*, Harper & Row, New York, 1962, p.26.

8   Merton, Thomas, *Love and Living*, p.36.

9   Ibid., p.166.

10 Quoted in Meyer, Eric D, "Giorgio Agamben. The Ominbus Homo Sacer," in *Philosophy Review*, Vol. XXXVIII, No. 3 (August 2018), p.85.

11 Gordon, George, *Byron, the Poetical Works of Lord Byron Complete in One Volume Collected and Arranged*, D. Appleton and Company, New York, 1853, p.63.

12 Schopenhauer, Arthur, *The Two Fundamental Problems of Ethics,* translated by D. E. Cartwright and E. E. Erdmann, Oxford University Press, New York, 1841, p.213.

13 Ibid., p.212.

14 Ibid.

15 Harris, Daniel I, "Compassion and Affirmation in Nietzsche," *Journal of Nietzsche Studies*, Vol. 48, No. 1 (Spring 2017), p.23.

16 Schopenhauer, Arthur, "The Foundation of Ethics," in *On the Basis of Morality* (1841) (translated by E. F. J. Payne), Bobbs-Merrill, Indianapolis, 1965, p.144.

144 *Notes*

17 Camus, Albert, "Why Spain?" in *Resistance, Rebellion and Death*, Alfred Knopf, Inc., New York, 1960, 1988, p.83.

18 Camus, Albert, "La Crise de l'Homme," in *Conferences et Discours* (1936–1958), Alfred Knopf, Paris, 2017, p.54.

19 His Holiness the XlVth Dalai Lama, Ramaswamy, India, 2006, p.148.

20 Camus, Albert, "Reflections on the Guillotine," in *Resistance, Rebellion and Death*, Alfred Knopf, Inc., New York, 1960, 1988, p.217.

21 Milton, John, "Paradise Lost," Book I, verse 260, in *Complete Poems and Major Prose*, The Odyssey Press, New York, 1957, p.218.

22 Althusser, Louis, "Man, That Night," in *The Spectre of Hegel: Early Writings* (translated by G. M. Goshgarian), Verso, London, 1997, p.170.

23 Kristjánsson, Kristján, "Pity: A Mitigated Defence," *Canadian Journal of Philosophy*, Vol. 44, No. 3/4 (June–August 2014), p.344.

24 Rousseau, Jean-Jacques, *Emile, or, on Education*, translated by A. Bloom, Basic Books, New York, 1979, p.221.

25 Beavers, Anthony F., "Desire and Love in Descartes's Late Philosophy," in *History of Philosophy Quarterly*, Vol. 6, No. 3 (July 1989), p.287.

26 Descartes, René, *The Passions of the Soul*, translated by Jonathan Bennett, 2017, p.52, at https://earlymoderntexts.com/assets/pdfs/descartes1649.pdf

27 Ibid.

28 Bicknell, Jeanette, "An Overlooked Aspect of Love in Spinoza's 'Ethics,'" *The Jerusalem Philosophical Quarterly*, 47 (January 1998), p.46.

29 Spinoza, Baruch, *Ethics and Selected Letters*, translated by Samuel Shirley, Hackett, Indianapolis, 1982, IV, 59S.

30 Bicknell, Jeanette, "An Overlooked Aspect," p.53.

31 Montaigne, *Essays*, translated by John Florio, edited by L. C. Harmer, 3 vols., Everyman's Library-Dent, London, 1965, Vol.1, p.18.

32 Shakespeare, William, *Coriolanus*, Act V Scene 3 in *The Complete Works*, Harcourt & World, New York, 1968, p.1311.

33 Ibid.

34 Naik, M. K., "Humanitarianism in Shakespeare," *Shakespeare Quarterly*, Vol. 19, No. 2 (Spring 1968), p.145.

Notes 145

35 Seneca, *De Clementia*, 2.4.4. in *Moral Essays*, translated by John W. Basore, Vol. 1, Harvard University Press, Cambridge, MA, 1994.

36 Sorabji, Richard, "When Was the Idea of Human Rights Invented, and Do We Need It?", at http://www.gresham.ac.uk/event. asp?PageId=45&EventId=78.

37 Cicero, "De Finibus" V 65, in *Annas* 1993:316–317.

38 Cochran, Elizabeth Agnew, "Virtuous Assent and Christian Faith: Retrieving Stoic Virtue Theory for Christian Ethics," *Journal of the Society of Christian Ethics*, Vol. 30, No. 1 (Spring/Summer 2010), p.120.

Chapter 1

1 Mukherji, Gangeya, "Exploring Non-violence: A Seminar Report," *Economic and Political Weekly*, Vol. 44, No. 24 (June 13–19, 2009), p.23.

2 Balslev, Anandita N., "Temple of Understanding: India and the US," *India International Centre Quarterly*, Vol. 42, No. 2 (Autumn 2015), p.112.

3 Dugar, B.R., "Gandhi and Jainism," *The Indian Journal of Political Science*, Vol. 74, No. 2 (April–June 2013), p.319.

4 Balslev, Anandita N., "Temple of Understanding: India and the US," p.112.

5 *The Dhammapada*, Chapter 14, translated by F. Max Muller, Routledge, London, 2013, p.51.

6 His Holiness the Dalai Lama, *Beyond Religion: Ethics for a Whole World*, HarperCollins, Noida, 2015, p.45.

7 Lecso, Phillip A., "To Do No Harm: A Buddhist View on Animal Use in Research," *Journal of Religion and Health*, Vol. 27, No. 4 (Winter 1988), p.310.

8 Barad, Judith, "The Understanding and Experience of Compassion: Aquinas and the Dalai Lama," *Buddhist-Christian Studies*, Vol. 27 (2007), p.13.

Notes

9   His Holiness the Dalai Lama, *Beyond Religion: Ethics for a Whole World*, pp.57–8.

10   Barad, Judith, "The Understanding and Experience of Compassion," pp.26–7.

11   Aguilar, Mario I., *The 14th Dalai Lama: Peacekeeping and Universal Responsibility*, Peacemakers Series, Routledge, London, 2021, p.26.

12   Richards, Glyn, *The Philosophy of Gandhi: A Study of His Basic Ideas*, Curzon Press, Totowa, 1982, p.33.

13   Weber, Max, *Political Writings*, edited by Peter Lassman and Ronald Speirs, Cambridge University Press, Cambridge, 1994, p.363.

14   Gandhi, Mahatma, *All Men Are Brothers*, edited by Krishna Kripalani, Navajivan Publishing House, Ahmedabad, 1971, p.126.

15   Ibid., p.171.

16   Ibid., p.108.

Chapter 2

1   See https://*www.bibliacatolica.com.br*/christian-community-bible/1-john/4/7.

2   https://*www.bibliacatolica.com.br*/christian-community-bible/matthew/5/7.

3   https://*www.bibliacatolica.com.br*/christian-community-bible/mark/6/34.

4   https://*www.bibliacatolica.com.br*/christian-community-bible/john/13/34.

5   https://*www.bibliacatolica.com.br*/christian-community-bible/luke/6/36.

6   Naseri, Christopher, "Reading Luke 15:11-32 as the Parable of Mercy and Compassion," *CABAN*, Vol. 9 (2017), pp.142–59.

7   https://www.bibliacatolica.com.br/christian-community-bible/matthew/5/43-44.

8   https://www.bibliacatolica.com.br/christian-community-bible/matthew/7/12.

9   Hurlbut, William B., "St. Francis, Christian Love, and the Biotechnological Future," *The New Atlantis*, No. 38 (Winter/Spring 2013), p.94.

Notes 147

10 Ibid., p.96.

11 Quoted in Ramakrishnan, Ram, *Many Paths, One Destination: Love, Peace, Compassion*, Wheatmark, Arizona, 2009, p.32.

12 Thomas of Celano, cited in Howell, A. G., trans., *The Lives of St. Francis of Assisi, by Brother Thomas of Celano*, n.p., New York, 1908, pp.57–9. Originally published as *Thomas of Celano, Vita prima sancti Francisci* 1.16.42–3, edited by E. d'Alencon, n.p., Rome, 1906.

13 Quoted in Helenius, Timo, *Ricoeur, Culture, and Recognition: A Hermeneutic of Cultural Subjectivity*, Lexington Books, Lanham, 2016, p.204.

14 Krishek, Sharon, "Two Forms of Love: The Problem of Preferential Love in Kierkegaard's 'Works of Love,'" *The Journal of Religious Ethics*, Vol. 36, No. 4 (December 2008), p.596.

15 Kierkegaard, Soren, *Works of Love*, p.238.

16 Ibid., pp.281–2.

17 Ibid., pp.23–4.

18 Ibid., pp.67–8.

19 Ibid., p.72.

20 Ibid., pp.143–4.

21 Ibid., pp.175–9.

22 Russell, Bertrand, *Autobiography*, Routledge, London, 2000, p.195.

23 Berlin, Isaiah, "Tolstoy and Enlightenment," in *Leo Tolstoy* (edited by Harold Bloom), Chelsea House, Philadelphia, 2003, p.29.

24 Steiner, Lina, "The Russian Aufklärer: Tolstoi in Search of Truth, Freedom, and Immortality," *Slavic Review*, Vol. 70, No. 4 (Winter 2011), pp.775, 777.

25 Buzhor, Vadim I., and Buzhor, Yevgenia, "The Ethical Conception of Leo Tolstoy in the Interpretation of Maximilian Voloshin," *SHS Web of Conferences*, Vol. 103, No. 01013 (2021), p.2.

26 Rabe, Ana Maria, "La Vida Está Fuera Del Tiempo. León Tolstói Entre La Práctica Vital Y La Predicación Moral," *ARBOR Ciencia, Pensamiento y Cultura* CLXXXVI 745, septiembre–octubre (2 0 1 0), p.952 (translated by the author).

148   *Notes*

27   O'Connell, Patrick F., "Keeping Pace with His Companion: Thomas Merton and Henry Thoreau," *The Concord Saunterer*, New Series, Vol. 7 (1999), p.130.

28   Ibid.

29   Merton, Thomas, *Learning to Love: Exploring Solitude and Freedom*, edited by Christine M. Bochen, HarperCollins, New York, 1998, p.315.

30   Gleeson, Denis, "'Meditation with Fireflies': An Introduction to Thomas Merton," *Studies: An Irish Quarterly Review*, Vol. 102, No. 405, John Bruton: What Would Happen if the EU Broke Up? (Spring 2013), p.49.

31   Labrie, Ross, "Contemplation and Action in Thomas Merton," *Christianity and Literature*, Vol. 55, No. 4 (Summer 2006), p.482.

32   Merton, Thomas, *Seeds of Destruction*, Farrar, Straus and Giroux, New York, 1964, p.xiii.

33   "Merton's Beliefs," *The Wilson Quarterly* (1976–), Vol. 10, No. 1 (New Year's 1986), p.28.

34   Labrie, Ross, "Contemplation and Action in Thomas Merton," p.490.

35   Merton, Thomas, *The Inner Experience: Notes on Contemplation*, edited by William H. Shannon, HarperCollins, San Francisco, 2003, p.73.

Chapter 3

1   Gandhi, Mahatma, *The Story of My Experiments with Truth: An Autobiography*, Lexicon Books, New Delhi, 2013, pp.136–7.

2   Ibid., pp.135–6.

3   Gandhi, Mahatma, *The Collected Works of Mahatma Gandhi*, Publications Division of the Government of India, New Delhi, 1958–1994, Vol. 20, p.404.

4   Gandhi, Mahatma, *The Essential Writings of Mahatma Gandhi*, edited by Raghavan Iyer, Oxford University Press of India, New Delhi, 2011, p.48.

5   Gandhi, Mahatma, *The Collected Works of Mahatma Gandhi*, p.27.

6   Gandhi, Mahatma, *All Men Are Brothers*, pp.107–8.

7   Ibid., pp.113–14.

Notes   149

8   Gandhi, Mahatma, *The Collected Works of Mahatma Gandhi*, pp.387–8.
9   Richards, Glyn, *The Philosophy of Gandhi*, p.71.
10   Gandhi, Mahatma, *All Men Are Brothers*, p.188.
11   Gupta, Ruchira, "Gandhi and Women in the Indian Freedom Struggle,"
     Social Scientist, Vol. 47, No. 1–2 (January–February 2019), p.38.
12   Gandhi, Mahatma, *All Men Are Brothers*, p.252.
13   Ibid., p.257.
14   Gandhi, Mahatma, *Selected Political Writings*, Hackett Publishing
     Company, Indianapolis, 1996, p.103.
15   Sarkar, Tanika, "Gandhi and Social Relations," in *The Cambridge
     Companion to Gandhi* (edited by Judith M. Brown and Anthony Parel),
     Cambridge University Press, Cambridge, 2011, p.185.
16   Gupta, Ruchira, "Gandhi and Women in the Indian Freedom Struggle,"
     p.41.
17   Patel, Sujata, "Construction and Reconstruction of Woman in Gandhi,"
     Economic and Political Weekly, Vol. 23, No. 8 (February 20, 1988),
     p.386.
18   Gandhi, Mahatma, *All Men Are Brothers*, pp.252–3.
19   Godse, Nathuram Vinayak, and Godse, Gopal Vinayak, *Why I
     Assassinated Mahatma Gandhi*, Surya Bharti Parkashan, Delhi, 1993,
     p.176.
20   Yadav, Yogendra, "Godse, Raised as a Girl, Saw Gandhi as an
     'effeminate' Father Who Didn't Protect Mother India," *The Print*,
     May 15, 2019.
21   Gandhi, Mahatma, *All Men Are Brothers*, p.199.
22   King, Martin Luther, Jr., *A Gift of Love*, foreword by Coretta Scott King,
     Penguin Books, UK, 2017, p.xvii.

Chapter 4

1   Johansen, Robert C., "Radical Islam and Nonviolence: A Case Study of
     Religious Empowerment and Constraint among Pashtuns," *Journal of
     Peace Research*, Vol. 34, No. 1 (February 1997), pp.60–1.

150 *Notes*

2 See Banerjee, Mukulika, *The Pathan Unarmed: Opposition and Memory in the North West Frontier*, Oxford University Press, London, 2000, p.13.

3 Ibid., p.34.

4 Bakshi, S. R., "Role Of Pathans in Civil Disobedience Movement 1930–34," *Proceedings of the Indian History Congress*, Vol. 42 (1981), p.479.

5 Tendulkar, D. G., *Abdul Ghaffar Khan: Faith Is a Battle*, Published for Gandhi Peace Foundation by Popular Prakashan, Bombay, 1967, pp.93–4.

6 Ahmad, Aijaz, "Frontier Gandhi: Reflections on Muslim Nationalism in India," *Social Scientist*, Vol. 33, No. 1/2 (January–February 2005), p.23.

7 Orakzai, Saira Bano, "Indigenous Cultural Resources for Peacebuilding," *International Journal of Conflict Engagement and Resolution*, Vol. 3, No. 2 (2015), p.189.

8 Ibid., p.192.

9 Bright, J.S., *Frontier and Its Gandhi*, Indian Printing Works, Lahore, 1944, pp.103–4.

10 Quoted in Jahanbegloo, Ramin, *The Clash of Intolerances*, Har-Anand Publications, New Delhi, 2007, pp.53–4.

11 Baldwin, James, "Letter from a Region in My Mind," *New Yorker*, November 17, 1962, p.6.

12 Quoted in Oates, Stephen B., *Let the Trumpet Sound: A Life of Martin Luther King Jr.*, Harper & Row, New York, 1982, p.32.

13 Frady, Marshall, *Martin Luther King, Jr.*, Viking, New York, 2002, pp.38–9.

14 King, Martin Luther, Jr., *Where Do We Go from Here: Chaos or Community?*", Beacon Press, Boston, 2010, p.198.

15 Birt, Robert E., "King's Radical Vision of Community," *https://www.academia.edu/ 31610171/* p.7.

16 King, Martin Luther Jr., *The Radical King*, edited by Cornel West, Beacon Press, Boston, 2015, p.XV.

17 Quoted in King, Martin Luther Jr., *A Gift of Love*, p.xvi.

18 King, Martin Luther Jr., *The Radical King*, p.158.

19 Ibid., pp.31–2.

20 King, Martin Luther Jr., *A Gift of Love*, pp.7–8.

Notes   151

21 Guth, Karen V., "Reconstructing Nonviolence: The Political Theology of Martin Luther King Jr. after Feminism and Womanism," *Journal of the Society of Christian Ethics*, Vol. 32, No. 1 (Spring/Summer 2012), p.77 (italics added by the author).

22 King, Martin Luther Jr., *In a Single Garment of Destiny: A Global Vision of Justice*, Beacon Press, Boston, 2012, p.149.

23 Ibid., p.132.

24 Martin Luther King, Jr., "Address before the National Bar Association," Milwaukee, Wisconsin (August 20, 1959), p.9., quoted in Baldwin, Lewis V., "Malcolm and Martin Luther King, JR.: What They Thought about Each Other," *Islamic Studies*, Vol. 25, No. 4 (Winter 1986), p.402.

25 King, Martin Luther Jr., *A Gift of Love*, p.154.

26 Frady, Marshall, *Martin Luther King, Jr.*, p.199.

Chapter 5

1 King, Martin Luther, Jr., *Why We Can't Wait*, Signet Classics, London, 2000, p.191.

2 King, Martin Luther, Jr., *Where Do We Go from Here*, pp.20–1.

3 Ibid., p.xx.

4 Gandhi, Mahatma, *The Collected Works of Mahatma Gandhi*, p.277.

5 Parel, Anthony, *Gandhi: Hind Swaraj and Other Writings*, Foundation Books, New Delhi, 1997, p.67.

6 Suhrud, Tridip, "Gandhi's Key Writings: In Search of Unity," in *The Cambridge Companion to Gandhi* (edited by Judith M. Brown and Anthony Parel), Cambridge University Press, Cambridge, 2011, p.73.

7 Ibid., p.74.

8 Gandhi, Mahatma, *All Men Are Brothers*, p.81.

9 See Parel, Anthony, *Gandhi*, p.73.

10 Gandhi, Mahatma, *Collected Works of Mahatma Gandhi*, Volume 42, Publications Division Government of India, New Delhi, 1999, p.22.

11 Fischer, Louis, *The Essential Gandhi: His Life, Work and Ideas*, Vintage Books, New York, 1963, p.197.

152   Notes

12   Iyer, Raghavan, *The Moral and Political Writings of Mahatma Gandhi*, Clarendon Press, tome III, Oxford, 1986, p.275.
13   Gandhi, Mahatma, *Selected Political Writings*, p.56.
14   Ibid., p.53.
15   King, Martin Luther Jr., "The Drum Major Instinct," in *A Time to Break Silence*, Beacon Press, Boston, 2013, pp.216–17.
16   King, Martin Luther Jr., *The Radical King*, p.4.
17   Ibid., pp.198–9.
18   Carson, Clayborne ed., *The Autobiography of Martin Luther King, Jr.*, Intellectual Properties Management in association with Warner Books, New York, 1998, p.339.
19   King, Martin Luther, Jr., *The Trumpet of Conscience*, Harper & Row, New York, 1968, p.69.
20   Iyer, Raghavan, *The Essential Writings of Mahatma Gandhi*, Oxford University Press, New Delhi, 2011, p.109.
21   Ibid., p.108.

Chapter 6

1   Easwaran, Eknath, *The Two Gandhis: Nonviolent Soldiers*, Jaico Publishing, Mumbai, 2009, p.174.
2   Boehmer, Elleke, *Nelson Mandela*, Sterling Publishing, New York, 2008, pp.96–7.
3   Ibid., p.185.
4   Ibid., p.186.
5   Tutu, Desmond Mpilo, *No Future without Forgiveness*, Double Day, New York, 1999, p.73.
6   Meredith, Martin, *Mandela: A Biography*, Simon& Schuster, London, 1997, p.564.
7   Eze, Chielozona, "Nelson Mandela and the Politics of Empathy: Reflections on the Moral Conditions for Conflict Resolutions in Africa," *African Conflict and Peacebuilding Review*, Vol. 2, No. 1 (Spring 2012), pp.123, 126.

Notes 153

8 Ibid., p.134.

9 Miller, sj., "Ubuntu: Calling in the Field," *English Education*, Vol. 48, No. 3 (April 2016), p.193.

10 Boehmer, Elleke, *Nelson Mandela*, pp.112–14.

11 Mandela, Nelson, *Long Walk to Freedom*, Abacus, London, 1994, p.680.

12 Mandela, Nelson, *Nelson Mandela: In His Own Words*, Little Brown and Company, New York, 2003, pp.345–6.

13 Mandela, Nelson, *Conversations with Myself*, Doubleday, Canada, 2010, p.382.

14 Mandela, Nelson, *Nelson Mandela*, pp.508–10.

15 Moosa, Ebrahim, "In Memoriam: Nelson Rolihlahla Mandela (1918–2013)," *Journal of the American Academy of Religion*, Vol. 82, No. 1 (March 2014), p.12.

16 Gandhi, Mahatma, *All Men Are Brothers*, p.267.

17 Mandela, Nelson, *Long Walk to Freedom*, p.751.

Conclusion

1 Critchley, Simon, *Notes on Suicide*, Fitzcarraldo editions, London, 2015, p.63.

2 Edman, Irwin, ed., *The Philosophy of Schopenhauer*, Modern Library, New York, 1956, p.343.

3 Quoted in Weil, Simone, *An Anthology*, Penguin Books, London, 2005, p.65.

4 Ibid., p.291.

5 Ibid., p.292.

6 Ibid., p.289.

7 Quoted in *The Confucian Four Books for Women*, translated by Ann A. Pang-White, Oxford University Press, Oxford, 2018, p.36.

8 Quoted in *The Indispensable Vivekananda: An Anthology for Our Times*, edited by Amita P. Sen, Permanent Black, Kolkata, 2006, p.148.

9 Quoted in *Readings in the Philosophy of Religion*, edited by Kelly James Clark, Broadview Press, Peterborough, 2017, p.433.

154 *Notes*

10 Quoted in *Nelson Mandela: Comparative Perspectives of His Significance for Education*, edited by Crain Soudien, Sense Publishers, Rotterdam, 2017, p.74.

11 Quoted in Todorov, Tzvetan, *The Conquest of America: The Question of the Other*, University of Oklahoma Press, Norman, 1999, p.167.

12 https://quoteinvestigator.com/2013/04/23/good-idea/.

13 Chardin, Teilhard de, *The Future of Man*, HarperCollins, London, 1964, p.125.

14 King, Martin Luther, Jr., *Where Do We Go from Here*, p.191.

15 Weil, Simone, *An Anthology*, p.103.

16 Radhakrishnan, Sarvepalli, *Faith Renewed*, Hind Pocket Books, Delhi, 2000, p.10.

17 Tagore, Rabindranath, My *Life in My Words*, Penguin Books, New Delhi, 2010, p.284.

18 Tagore, Rabindranath, *Selected Letters of Rabindranath Tagore*, Cambridge University Press, Cambridge, 1997, p.515.

19 Berlin, Isaiah, "Rabindranath Tagore and the Consciousness of Nationality," in *The Sense of Reality: Studies in Ideas and Their History*, Farrar, Straus and Giroux, New York, 1997, p.265.

20 Tagore, Rabindranath, "Sadhana," in *Selected Essays*, Rupa&Co., New Delhi, 2010, p.155

21 Ibid.

22 Ibid., p.137.

23 Tagore, Rabindranath, "Creative Unity," in *Selected Essays*, Rupa&Co., New Delhi, 2010, p.11.

24 Tagore, Rabindranath, *Personality*, Macmillan, New York, 1948, p.14.

25 Tagore, Rabindranath, *Inspiring Thoughts*, Rajpal&Sons, Delhi, 2013, p.18.

26 Tagore, Rabindranath, "Sadhana," pp.155–6.

27 Tagore, Rabindranath, "The Religion of Man," in *Selected Essays*, Rupa&Co., New Delhi, 2010, p.382.

28 Tagore, Rabindranath, "Message to the Parliament of Religions," in *Selected Essays*, Rupa&Co., New Delhi, 2010, p.315.

29 Tagore, Rabindranath, "Creative Unity," p.73.

Notes 155

30 Tagore, Rabindranath, "Crisis in Civilisation," in *Selected Essays*, Rupa&Co., New Delhi, 2010, p.268.

31 Tagore, Rabindranath, *Inspiring Thoughts*, p.19.

32 Ghose, Aurobindo, *The Hour of God: Selections from His Writings*, Sahitya Akademi, New Delhi, 1995, p.66.

33 Quoted in Krinsky, Santosh, *Readings in Sri Aurobindo's the Human Cycle*, Lotus Press, Twin Lakes, 2019, p.138.

34 Quoted in Kealey, A. Daniel, *Revisioning Environmental Ethics*, State University of New York Press, New York, 1990, p.82.

35 Ghose, Aurobindo, *The Ideal of Human Unity*, Sri Aurobindo Ashram, Pondicherry, 1950, p.50.

36 Quoted in Krinsky, Santosh, *Readings in Sri Aurobindo's the Human Cycle*, p.128.

37 Quoted in Richards, Glyn ed., *A Source-Book of Modern Hinduism*, Curzon Press, Surrey, 1996, p.148.

38 Ghose, Aurobindo, "The Awakening Soul of India," in *Speeches and Writings of Eminent Indians*, Macmillan and Co Limited, 1952, at https://nationalistspeeches.wordpress.com/2019/11/27/sri-aurobindo-the-awakening-soul-of-india/.

39 Quoted in Hardiman, David, *The Nonviolent Struggle for Indian Freedom, 1905–19*, Oxford University Press, Oxford, 2018, p.36.

40 Ghose, Aurobindo, "Bande Mataram. April 9, 1908," at https://www.aurobindo.ru/workings/sa/01/0309_e.htm.

41 Quoted in http://egyankosh.ac.in/bitstream/123456789/35736/1/Unit-4.pdf.

42 Quoted in "Auroville: Aurobindo's City of Global Unity," *The UNESCO Courier*, 1972, p.10.

43 Quoted in Jugal Kishore Mukherjee, *Sri Aurobindo International Centre of Education*, University of Michigan Press, Michigan, 1990, p.202.

44 Ghose, Aurobindo, *The Essential Aurobindo*, Lindisfarne Books, MA, 1987, p.64.

45 Quoted in Sharma, Chandradhar, *A Critical Survey of Indian Philosophy*, Motilal Banarsidass Publishers, Delhi, 1987, p.384.

156 *Notes*

46 Quoted in Heehs, Peter, "Sri Aurobindo and His Ashram, 1910–2010: An Unfinished History," *Nova Religio: The Journal of Alternative and Emergent Religions*, Vol. 19, No. 1 (August 2015), p.71.

47 Quoted in Chandra, Soti Shivandra, and Sharma, Rajendra Kumar, *Principles of Education*, Atlantic Publishers, New Delhi, 2004, p.223.

48 Krinsky, Santosh, *Readings in Sri Aurobindo's the Human Cycle*, p.60.

49 Quoted in Ghose, Aurobindo, *Ārya: A Philosophical Review*, Volume 2, All India Books, Sri Aurobindo's Ashram, 1990, p.761.

50 Joshi, V.C., *Sri Aurobindo: An Interpretation*, Nehru Memorial Library, New Delhi, 1973, p.146.

51 Mohanty, Sachidananda, *Sri Aurobindo: A Contemporary Reader*, Routledge, New Delhi, 2008, p.88.

52 Quoted in Kishore, Kaushal, *The Life and Times of Sri Aurobindo Ghosh*, Ocean Books, New Delhi, 2016, p.123.

53 Quoted in Heehs, Peter, *The Lives of Sri Aurobindo*, Columbia University Press, New York, 2008, p.403.

54 Mohanty, Sachidananda, *Sri Aurobindo: A Contemporary Reader*, p.70.

55 Gandhi, Mahatma, *Selected Political Writings*, p.106.

56 Gandhi, Mahatma, *My Nonviolence*, Navajivan Publishing House, Ahmedabad, 1960, p.37–8.

57 Ibid., p.227.

58 King, Martin Luther, Jr., *A Testament of Hope*, edited by James M. Washington, Harper One, New York, 1986, p.242.

59 Gandhi, Mahatma, *My Nonviolence*, p.84.

60 King, Martin Luther, Jr., *A Testament of Hope*, p.9.

61 Shakespeare, William, *Arden Shakespeare Complete Works*, edited by Ann Thompson, David Scott Kastan, Bloomsbury, London, 2014, p.42.

Bibliography

Aguilar, Mario I., *The 14th Dalai Lama: Peacekeeping and Universal Responsibility*, Peacemakers Series, Routledge, London, 2021.

Althusser, Louis, *The Spectre of Hegel: Early Writings*, translated by G. M. Goshgarian, Verso, London, 1997.

Banerjee, Mukulika, *The Pathan Unarmed: Opposition and Memory in the North West Frontier*, Oxford University Press, London, 2000.

Berlin, Isaiah, *The Sense of Reality: Studies in Ideas and Their History*, Farrar, Straus and Giroux, New York, 1997.

Boehmer, Elleke, *Nelson Mandela*, Sterling Publishing, New York, 2008.

Bloom, Harold (ed.), *Leo Tolstoy*, Chelsea House, Philadelphia, 2003.

Brown, Judith M, and Parel, Anthony, *The Cambridge Companion to Gandhi*, Cambridge University Press, Cambridge, 2011.

Camus, Albert, "Reflections on the Guillotine," in *Resistance, Rebellion and Death*, Alfred Knopf, Inc., New York, 1960.

Camus, Albert, "Why Spain?" in *Resistance, Rebellion and Death*, Alfred Knopf, New York, 1960.

Camus, Albert, *Conferences et Discours* (1936–1958), Folio-Gallimard, Paris, 2017.

Carson, Clayborne (ed.), *The Autobiography of Martin Luther King, Jr.*, Intellectual Properties Management in association with Warner Books, New York, 1998.

Celano, Thomas, *The Lives of St. Francis of Assisi, by Brother Thomas of Celano*, n.p., New York, 1908.

Chandra, Soti Shivandra, and Sharma, Rajendra Kumar, *Principles of Education*, Atlantic Publishers, New Delhi, 2004.

Chardin, Teilhard de, *The Future of Man*, HarperCollins, London, 1964.

Clark, Kelly James (ed.), *Readings in the Philosophy of Religion*, Broadview Press, Peterborough, 2017.

Critchley, Simon, *Notes on Suicide*, Fitzcarraldo editions, London, 2015.

The Dhammapada, translated by F. Max Muller, Routledge, London, 2013.

Descartes, René, *The Passions of the Soul*, translated by Jonathan Bennett, 2017.

158 *Bibliography*

Easwaran, Eknath, *The Two Gandhis: Nonviolent Soldiers*, Jaico Publishing, Mumbai, 2009.

Edman, Irwin (ed.), *The Philosophy of Schopenhauer*, Modern Library, New York, 1956.

Fischer, Louis, *The Essential Gandhi: His Life, Work and Ideas*, Vintage Books, New York, 1963.

Frady, Marshall, *Martin Luther King, Jr.*, Viking, New York, 2002.

Fromm, Erich, *The Art of Loving*, Harper & Row, New York, 1962.

Gandhi, Mahatma, *The Collected Works of Mahatma Gandhi*, Publications Division of the Government of India, New Delhi, 1958–1994, 100 volumes.

Gandhi, Mahatma, *My Nonviolence*, Navajivan Publishing House, Ahmedabad, 1960.

Gandhi, Mahatma, *All Men Are Brothers*, edited by Krishna Kripalani, Navajivan Publishing House, Ahmedabad, 1971.

Gandhi, Mahatma, *Selected Political Writings*, Hackett Publishing, Indianapolis, 1996.

Gandhi, Mahatma, *The Story of My Experiments with Truth: An Autobiography*, Lexicon Books, New Delhi, 2013.

Ghose, Aurobindo, *The Ideal of Human Unity*, Sri Aurobindo Ashram, Pondicherry, 1950.

Ghose, Aurobindo, *The Essential Aurobindo*, Lindisfarne Books, MA, 1987.

Ghose Aurobindo, *The Hour of God: Selections from His Writings*, Sahitya Akademi, New Delhi, 1995.

Godse, Nathuram Vinayak, and Godse, Gopal Vinayak, *Why I Assassinated Mahatma Gandhi*, Surya Bharti Parkashan, Delhi, 1993.

Gordon, George, *Byron, the Poetical Works of Lord Byron Complete in One Volume Collected and Arranged*, D. Appleton and Company, New York, 1853.

Hardiman, David, *The Nonviolent Struggle for Indian Freedom, 1905–19*, Oxford University Press, Oxford, 2018.

Heehs, Peter, *The Lives of Sri Aurobindo*, Columbia University Press, New York, 2008.

Helenius, Timo, *Ricoeur, Culture, and Recognition: A Hermeneutic of Cultural Subjectivity*, Lexington Books, Lanham, 2016.

Bibliography

His Holiness the Dalai Lama, *Beyond Religion: Ethics for a Whole World*, HarperCollins, Noida, 2015.

Iyer, Raghavan, *The Essential Writings of Mahatma Gandhi*, Oxford University Press, New Delhi, 2011.

Joshi, V. C., *Sri Aurobindo: An Interpretation*, Nehru Memorial Library, New Delhi, 1973.

Kealey, A. Daniel, *Revisioning Environmental Ethics*, State University of New York Press, New York, 1990.

Kierkegaard, Soren, *Works of Love*, Harper & Row, New York, 1962.

Kierkegaard, Soren, *The Essential Kierkegaard*, Princeton University Press, Princeton, 1997.

King, Martin Luther, Jr., *The Trumpet of Conscience*. Harper & Row, New York, 1968.

King, Martin Luther, Jr., *A Testament of Hope*, edited by James M. Washington, Harper One, New York, 1986.

King, Martin Luther, Jr., *Why We Can't Wait*, Signet Classics, London, 2000, 191.

King, Martin Luther, Jr., *Where Do We Go From Here: Chaos or Community?*, Beacon Press, Boston, 2010.

King, Martin Luther Jr., *In a Single Garment of Destiny: A Global Vision of Justice*, Beacon Press, Boston, 2012.

King, Martin Luther Jr., *A Time to Break Silence*, Boston, Beacon Press, 2013.

King, Martin Luther Jr., *The Radical King*, edited by Cornel West, Beacon Press, Boston, 2015.

King, Martin Luther, *A Gift of Love*, foreword by Coretta Scott King, Penguin Books, UK, 2017.

Kishore, Kaushal, *The Life and Times of Sri Aurobindo Ghosh*, Ocean Books, New Delhi, 2016.

Krinsky, Santosh, *Readings in Sri Aurobindo's: The Human Cycle*, Lotus Press, Twin Lakes, 2019.

Kundera, Milan, *The Unbearable Lightness of Being*, Harper & Row, New York, 1984.

Mandela, Nelson, *Long Walk to Freedom*, Abacus, London, 1994.

Mandela, Nelson, *Nelson Mandela: In His Own Words*, Little Brown and Company, New York, 2003.

160 *Bibliography*

Mandela, Nelson, *Conversations with Myself*, Doubleday, Canada, 2010.

Marcuse, Herbert, *Eros and Civilization*, Beacon Press, Boston, 1966.

Meredith, Martin, *Mandela: A Biography*, Simon & Schuster, London, 1997.

Merton, Thomas, *Seeds of Destruction*, Farrar, Straus and Giroux, New York, 1964.

Merton, Thomas, *Love and Living*, A Harvest/HBJ Book, New York, 1985.

Merton, Thomas, *Learning to Love: Exploring Solitude and Freedom*, edited by Christine M. Bochen, HarperCollins, New York, 1998.

Merton, Thomas, *The Inner Experience: Notes on Contemplation*, edited by William H. Shannon, HarperCollins, San Francisco, 2003.

Milton, John, *Complete Poems and Major* Prose, The Odyssey Press, New York, 1957.

Mohanty, Sachidananda, *Sri Aurobindo: A Contemporary Reader*, Routledge, New Delhi, 2008.

Montaigne, *Essays*, translated by John Florio, edited by L. C. Harmer, 3 vols., Everyman's Library-Dent, London, 1965.

Mukherjee, Jugal Kishore, *Sri Aurobindo International Centre of Education*, University of Michigan Press, Michigan, 1990.

Oates, Stephen B., *Let the Trumpet Sound: A Life of Martin Luther King Jr.*, Harper & Row, New York, 1982.

Parel, Anthony, *Gandhi: Hind Swaraj and Other Writings*, Foundation Books, New Delhi, 1997.

Radhakrishnan, Sarvepalli, *Faith Renewed*, Hind Pocket Books, Delhi, 2000.

Ramakrishnan, Ram, *Many Paths, One Destination: Love, Peace, Compassion*, Wheatmark, Arizona, 2009.

Richards, Glyn, *The Philosophy of Gandhi: A Study of His Basic Ideas*, Curzon Press, Totowa, 1982.

Richards, Glyn (ed.), *A Source-Book of Modern Hinduism*, Curzon Press, Surrey, 1996.

Rousseau, Jean-Jacques, *Emile, or, on Education*, translated by A. Bloom, Basic Books, New York, 1979.

Russell, Bertrand, *Autobiography*, Routledge, London, 2000.

Schopenhauer, Arthur, *The Two Fundamental Problems of Ethics,* translated by D. E. Cartwright and E. E. Erdmann, Oxford University Press, New York, 1841.

Bibliography

Schopenhauer, Arthur, "The Foundation of Ethics," in *On the Basis of Morality* (1841), translated by E. F. J. Payne, Bobbs-Merrill, Indianapolis, 1965.

Seneca, *Moral Essays*, translated by John W. Basore, Vol. 1, Harvard University Press, Cambridge, MA, 1994.

Shakespeare, William, *The Complete Works*, Harcourt & World, New York, 1968.

Sharma, Chandradhar, *A Critical Survey of Indian Philosophy*, Motilal Banarsidass Publishers, Delhi, 1987.

Soudien, Crain (ed.), Nelson *Mandela: Comparative Perspectives of His Significance for Education*, Sense Publishers, Rotterdam, 2017.

Spinoza, Baruch, *Ethics and Selected Letters*, translated by Samuel Shirley, Hackett, Indianapolis, 1982.

Tagore, Rabindranath, *Personality*, Macmillan, New York, 1948.

Tagore, Rabindranath, Selected *Letters of Rabindranath Tagore*, Cambridge University Press, Cambridge, 1997.

Tagore, Rabindranath, My *Life in My Words*, Penguin Books, New Delhi, 2010.

Tagore, Rabindranath, *Selected Essays*, Rupa & Co., New Delhi, 2010.

Tagore, Rabindranath, *Inspiring Thoughts*, Rajpal & Sons, Delhi, 2013.

Tendulkar, Dinanath Gopal, *Abdul Ghaffar Khan: Faith Is a Battle*, Published for Gandhi Peace Foundation by Popular Prakashan, Bombay, 1967.

Todorov, Tzvetan, *The Conquest of America: The Question of the Other*, University of Oklahoma Press, Norman, 1999.

Tutu, Desmond Mpilo, *No Future without Forgiveness*, Double Day, New York, 1999.

Weber, Max, *Political Writings*, edited by Peter Lassman, and Ronald Speirs, Cambridge University Press, Cambridge, 1994.

Weil, Simone, *An Anthology*, Penguin Books, London, 2005.

Index

A
advaita 61
African National Congress (ANC) 105, 106
Althusser, Louis 10
ascetic life 19
Aurobindo 128
  on Asia 131
  Bande Mataram 130
  education 134
  The Ideal of Human Unity 129
  The Life Divine 128
  on Man 133
  Saccidananda 129
  sanatana dharma 130
  Supermind 133
  uniformity 136
Azad Islamia Madrassa 72

B
Badshah Khan 73
beatitudes 34, 36
Berlin, Isaiah 121
Bhagavad-Gita 28, 31
bliss 133
Buddha 20, 57, 61
Buddhist doctrine 24
Buddhist ethics 16

C
Camus, Albert 9, 10
Chardin, Teilhard de 118
Chatvari-arya-satyani. See Four Noble Truths
Christ
  Sermon on the Mount 49
christian love 42, 48, 54, 113
Christian nonviolence 34, 41, 49, 53
Cicero 15, 16

compassionate love 11, 12, 31, 43, 46
compassionate man 12
compromise 58, 105, 128
condition sine qua non 57
Confucius 115
contemplation 52, 53, 54
controversy of Valladolid 117
Cornel West 79

D
Dalai Lama 10, 25, 70
death 113
Descartes, Rene 11, 116
The Dhammapada 24
dharma 21, 23, 29, 128
Dharma Prabhavana 21

E
eleos 11
empathetic pluralism 59
evil 11
examined lives 98

F
Finis Origine Pendet 115
Four Noble Truths 20

G
Gandhi 5, 23, 51, 125
  on Buddha 57
  on christianity 56
  compassionate humanity 137
  criticizing modern civilization 87
  defining civilization 86
  electoral liberalism 68
  empathetic pluralism 59
  ethical citizenship 89
  feminine view of nonviolent organization 68

Index

feminization of Indian politics 65
Gandhian *satyagraha* 76
Hind Swaraj 86
idea of a compassionate
    civilization 88
Is Nonviolence Ineffective 139
letter to de Manziarly 99
Mahatma 69
means and ends 88
otherness of the Other 89
Pathan Red Shirts 73
project of civilization 88
quest for Truth 88
self-examination 87
self-governing agents 89
Socratic approach 87
spiritualization of politics 97
structural violence 118
swaraj 90
the Self and the Other 91
Tolstoy 55
Gautama. *See* Buddha
generositas. See nobility
Gita. See Bhagavad-Gita
golden rule 37
Gospel spirituality 52

H
hic et nunc 57
Hinduism
    caste system 20
    Godse 67
    shared humanity 28
homo fragilis 141
Homo sacra reshomini 7
humaneness 115
humanness 85

I
incarnational spirituality 52
Indian civilization 60, 137
infinite debt 47, 48
inter-faith dialogue 58, 73
inwardization of the world 124

J
Jain morality 22
Jesus of Nazareth 114
jina 21

K
Karma 22, 24
karma yogin 60
karuna 19, 23
Khan, Abdul Ghaffar. 85, 136
    Anjuman-i-Islah-ul-Afaghana 72
    ethicization of politics 74
    involving women 71
    Khudai Khidmatgar 70
    nonviolence as an article of faith 72
    proponent of nonviolence 70
    self-restraint 73
    soft reading of Islam 77
Kierkegaard, Soren
    eternity of love 45
    neighborly love 44
    suffering 43
    Works of Love 42
King, Martin Luther, Jr., 76, 85, 95, 118
    Agape love 77
    Autobiography 76
    Beloved Community 97, 138
    compassionate interdependence 80
    cosmic companionship 80
    Gandhian nonviolence 84
    Gandhian Satyagraha 82
    Kingian moral attitude 78
    Montgomery Bus Boycott 80
    radical compassion 79
    Satyagraha as philosophy of
        praxis 76
    satyagrahi 81
    Vietnam War 96
    World house 83
Kundera, Milan 3

L
Las Casas, Bartolomé de 116, 117
Las Casas-Sepúlveda controversy 118

164 *Index*

liberation. *See* Moksha
Lord Byron 7, 143, 158

M
Mahavira 21, 68, 140
Mahayana. *See* Mahayana Buddhism
Mahayana Buddhism 25
Mandela, Nelson 116
    compassionate fellowship 101
    epistemic humility 103
    gandhian phases 105
    Long Walk to Freedom 106
    otherness of the Other 102
    re-humanizing 103
    sharing together 104
    speech at Gandhi Hall 106
Marcuse, Herbert 4, 143
mercy 15, 33, 60, 141
Merton, Thomas 2, 5, 37, 51, 52
    Seeds of Destruction 53
Mikhailovsky 48
Moksha 30
Montaigne, Michel de 14
Mundi, Amor 3, 119

N
Nathuram Godse 67
neighborly love 42, 45
New Testament 33, 51, 56
Nietzsche 9
Nirvana 24, 30
nobility 13
nonviolence 62, 73, 74

O
oikeiosis 15
Old Testament 36
outwardization of the self 123

P
preferential love 42, 43, 45, 46
Prospero 14

R
Radhakrishnan, Sarvepalli 120
responsible love 43

S
Sachchidananda. See bliss
sacrifice. *See* yajna
satyagrahi 56, 64, 93
Schopenhauer, Arthur
    fundamental metaphysics of
      loving 114
    homo fragilis and suffering 7
    love as affirmation of will to live
      113
    The Self 115
    self-sacrifice 57
Seneca 7, 15, 16
Sepúlveda 117, 118
Shakespeare, William 14, 15, 141
solitude 38, 52
Spinoza, Baruch 13
spiritual wells 58
St. Francis 37
    Basilica of Santa Maria degli
      Angeli 39
    Canticle of the Creatures 42
    church of *San Damiano* 38
    early life 38
    evangelical experience 37
    love as founding principle 40
    Rome 39
    spiritual message 41
    Testament 42
Stoic 15, 16
structural violence 118
Swami Vivekananda 115

T
Tagore, Rabindranath 120
    compassionate civilization 120
    compassionate fellowship 120
    love for God 125
    otherness of the Other 121
    Santiniketan 126
    the spirit of Man 127
    two concepts 124
    universal compassion 122
Tagore's letter to Leonard Elmhirst
    121
tapasya. See self-sacrifice

Index

Thomas of Celano 40, 41
Tibetan Buddhism 26, 27
Tolstoy
    *The Kingdom of God is within
      you* 51
Tolstoy, Leo 65
    apostle of nonviolence 48
    evil 49
    Pascal 49
    War and Peace 49
TRC. *See* Truth and Reconciliation
    Commission
Truth and Reconciliation
    Commission 103
Tutu, Desmond 34, 70, 103

U
ubuntu 105
Ubuntu. *See* Ubuntu Philosophy

Ubuntu philosophy 102
Umkhonto we Sizwe 105
Upanishads 29, 125

V
vartas 22
a vice of the mind. *See* vitium animi
the virtue of non-contention 116
vitium animi 15

W
by way of comparison 48
Weil, Simone 37, 113, 114, 119

Y
yajna 56

Z
Zeitgeist 98

Printed in the USA
CPSIA information can be obtained
at www.ICGtesting.com
LVHW050320020624
781922LV00002B/223